WILLIAM SHIPLEY

Founder of
the Royal Society of Arts

A BIOGRAPHY WITH DOCUMENTS

D.G.C. ALLAN

FOREWORD BY HIS ROYAL HIGHNESS
THE PRINCE PHILIP, DUKE OF EDINBURGH K.G. K.T.
PRESIDENT OF THE ROYAL SOCIETY OF ARTS

HUTCHINSON OF LONDON

HUTCHINSON & CO (*Publishers*) LTD
178–202 Great Portland Street, London W1

London Melbourne Sydney
Auckland Bombay Toronto
Johannesburg New York

First published 1968

*This book has been set in Garamond, printed in Great Britain
on Antique Wove paper by Anchor Press, and
bound by Wm. Brendon, both of Tiptree, Essex*

09 085700 3

CONTENTS

CONTENTS

ILLUSTRATIONS

ILLUSTRATIONS

In memory
M.A.A.

ACKNOWLEDGEMENTS

My first thanks are to the Council of the Royal* Society of Arts, both for permission to quote freely from the Society's Mss. records and printed proceedings, and for encouragement to undertake research into the early history of the Society as part of my work as Curator-Librarian of the Society. The willing spokesmen of this encouragement have been Mr. G. E. Mercer, sixteenth Secretary of the Society since William Shipley's time, and Mr. J. S. Skidmore, Editor of the *Journal of the Royal Society of Arts*. When parts of this study were printed in the Society's *Journal* (Vols. CXIII, CXIV and CXV, 1965-7) Mr. Skidmore read them through and made many helpful criticisms and he has now done the same for the remainder of the work.

The generous permission which the American Philosophical Society, the John Rylands Library, the Royal Academy and the Royal Society have given me to print various manuscripts in their possession has been acknowledged in appropriate footnotes and references. Through the courtesy of their owners, I have been allowed to include amongst my illustrations the mezzotint of *A Boy Blowing a Firebrand* (Trustees of the British Museum), the photographs of Twyford House (Messrs. James Harris & Son, Winchester), of Craig's Court (Greater London Council, Photographic Library), and of Knightrider House (Maidstone and District Motor Services Ltd.); the portrait(s) by Shipley and Lord Romney and the drawings by Shipley's pupils (the Royal Society of Arts); and the engraving of Ozias Humphry (National Portrait Gallery).

I have acknowledged the specific assistance of several scholars by name in Chapter 1 and in the notes. I have also received valuable help and advice of a general character from

* The prefix 'Royal' was not used in Shipley's time. It dates from 1908.

ACKNOWLEDGEMENTS

Mr. Lionel Alroy, Dr. Whitfield J. Bell, *Jnr.*, Mr. Maurice Butler, F.R.S.A., Miss M. B. C. Canney, Mrs. E. Cottrill, Mr. Hugh Clausen, O.B.E., F.R.S.A., Mr. James Harrison, F.R.S.A., Mrs. Hilda Jaffa, Mr. C. W. Kellaway, Professor R. E. Schofield, F.R.S.A., and Professor J. B. Shipley.

Lastly, since the publisher has a right to the final word, let me thank Mr. Thomas Dalby, F.R.S.A., of Hutchinson and Co. for much help and kindness.

D.G.C.A.

FOREWORD

People who are capable of creating something are always interesting. Whether William Shipley appreciated the magnitude and importance of the creation of the Royal Society of Arts is uncertain but I think he would be entitled to a modest glow of pride if he could see the activities of the Society today.

Mr. Allan has put together a most illuminating volume about a man who was at the centre of much philanthropic work and deeply involved in the encouragement of the Arts during the most exciting years of the eighteenth century.

1968

CHRONOLOGY

1715   William Shipley baptised on 2nd June at St. Stephen's, Walbrook

1719   Jonathan Shipley, father of W.S., dies. W.S. becomes the responsibility of his maternal grandfather, William Davies, *Snr.*, of Twyford House, Hants

1727   Death of William Davies, *Snr.*

1736   W.S. attains age of 21 and receives £500 under wil of William Davies, *Snr.*

1747–53   W.S. at Northampton. Practises as a painter and drawing master, joins Northampton Philosophical Society, raises fund to buy fuel for poor

1753   W.S. publishes his *Proposals* and *Scheme* for a Society of Arts

1754   Foundation of Society of Arts and of 'Shipley's School' in London

1755–60   Secretary and Register of Society of Arts. Elected to Life Membership and awarded Gold Medal as Founder

1760–8   First period as a frequent attender at Society of Arts Committees

1762   Schemes for Repository of Arts and Fishery Development

1765   Death of William Davies, *Jnr.*, who leaves £1,000 to his nephew W.S.

1767   W.S. marries Elizabeth Miller at St. George's, Hanover Square, on 23rd November

1768   W.S. settles at Maidstone, Kent, where he remains until his death

1769   First child, Elizabeth, born but dies after two months

1771   Second child, Elizabeth, born

1772   W.S. attends at a Committee of Society of Arts for first time since 1768

1777   Receives Silver Medal from Society of Arts for his floating light

1778–87 Second period as frequent attender at Society of Arts Committees. Submits several inventions to Society and prepares a scheme for educational reform

1783–7   Active as Treasurer of the Society for Promoting Useful Knowledge, Maidstone

1786   Publishes his *Proposal* for expanding the Maidstone Society into a Kentish Society for Promoting Useful Knowledge, and undertakes a successful canvass for this purpose

1788   Death of Jonathan Shipley, Bishop of St. Asaph, elder brother of W.S.

1789–90 W.S. suffers under illness

1792–6   Fellow of Linnean Society, but cannot come to London to attend its meetings

1795   Member of Governing Committee of a new Kentish Society

1803   'Tribute of Respect' paid to W.S. at Society of Arts Prize-giving on 1st July. W.S. dies at Maidstone on 28th December

I

INTRODUCTION

'William Shipley . . . lui dont j'aurois voulu voir le nom dans le Plutarque anglois.'

P. N. Chantreau, *Voyage dans les trois royaumes d'Angleterre, d'Ecosse et d'Irlande*, 1792

---

[a] *The biographical problem*

In his *History of the Royal Society of Arts*, which was published in 1913, Sir Henry Trueman Wood noted that 'the materials for a life of Shipley are scanty',[1] and the sources he listed have formed the basis of all subsequent accounts of the life of the Founder of the Society. Hudson and Luckhurst's admirable bicentenary history of the Society[2] stimulated interest in William Shipley's achievement when it appeared in 1954 but could add nothing to Trueman Wood's list. In 1958 the present writer completed a catalogue of the Society's early archives and during the years that followed a number of English and American scholars published monographs on fresh aspects of the Society's history.[3] Techniques were developed for using the Society's minutes and membership lists in biographical studies which made it certain that much could be learnt of Shipley's fifty-year-long association with the Society if time could be found to apply them to his case. A further induce-ment to attempt his biography was the discovery of several letters from Shipley to the Society which had been overlooked by its previous historians. Yet his life before the foundation of the Society remained a mystery and not much more was known about his years in Maidstone.

The best known source for the pre-history of the Society of Arts is Thomas Mortimer's *Concise Account*, which was published in 1763 as the printed version of a now vanished manuscript of 1758. Mortimer traces the evolution of Shipley's scheme to stimulate artistic and scientific skills by competitions for prizes, and from his narrative are derived the familiar stories of the founder's interest in the Northampton horse fairs and of his successful struggle with the local fuel profiteers during the winters of 1751 and 1752. Shipley's local successes encouraged him to persevere with his plan to form a national society for the public good, and Mortimer states that he was advised to try it out in London by 'some ingenious and public spirited gentlemen in the neighbourhood'. His London contacts were limited to three acquaintances who might be 'capable of forwarding his design', including Henry Baker, the microscopist, and 'He had also a recommendation to the Reverend Dr. Stephen Hales of Teddington.'[4]

An enlargement of Mortimer's narrative was attempted first through a study of Hales, who because of his fame as a scientist seemed most likely to be the best documented figure, and though no correspondence between Hales and Shipley has survived a link between them was found in Thomas Yeoman, an engineer and friend of Hales who turned out to be the President of a philosophical society at Northampton, to which Shipley said in one of his letters in the Society of Arts' archives that he had once belonged. Mr. Eric Robinson, a modern authority on Thomas Yeoman and the Northampton Philosophical Society,[5] then supplied references to some letters about that Society exchanged between Dr. Doddridge, the celebrated Northampton Dissenting Minister and Henry Baker, which are preserved in the Baker collection at the John Rylands Library in Manchester.[6] Work on this collection revealed holograph letters from Shipley to Baker written during the crucial years 1749 and 1753, which contain references to the genesis of the Society of Arts and several significant clues regarding the character and interests of their author.

The Baker letters presented Shipley as a man in early middle-age well versed in scientific and antiquarian learning and yet apparently too modest to claim Fellowship of either the Royal or Antiquarian Societies where Baker himself had so much influence. They show he had the leisure to pursue schemes for the public welfare but say nothing of his financial or family circumstances. To reconstruct the first thirty-four years of his life a lengthy search was necessary amongst wills and parish registers. Fortunately both encouragement and assistance was received from Miss K. M. Kenyon, a Fellow of the Royal Society of Arts, who resides in Twyford village, Hampshire, where Shipley spent his boyhood years. Miss Kenyon not only drew on her own extensive knowledge of the history of the village but obtained permission from Mrs. M. Dykes, the present owner of Twyford Moors,[7] so that an inspection might be made of the Shipley muniments. In 1964 the writer was most hospitably entertained by Mrs. Dykes at Twyford Moors and given complete freedom to work on the family papers.

After the pattern of his family background had been established the next subject of enquiry was Shipley's professional activity as an artist and a search was begun for some work of his brush. Edward Edwards, Horace Walpole's successor as the historian of British Art, writing before 1808 referred to a 'Mezzotinto print by Faber of a boy blowing a firebrand marked with the name of Shipley as the painter', and his statement was repeated by Redgrave and later dictionaries of artists.[8] But attempts to locate the print in the British Museum on the basis of this information proved unsuccessful and widespread enquiries addressed to other collections and published in the press yielded no result. It was not until a visit had been paid to the Maidstone Museum and Art Gallery that some progress was made towards a solution of the mystery. At Maidstone there was displayed an oil painting entitled 'Boy blowing a brand', attributed to the Dutch artist Godfreid Schalcken (1643–1706). The name Schalcken was thought to have been confused with Shipley, and a previous Curator of the Museum had erased from his notes the statement that the painting was by Shipley, though he had noted the oral evidence of a descendant of one of Shipley's servants that it had once been in the possession of Shipley's family at Knightrider House, Maidstone.[9] However, a renewed search at the British Museum, this time guided by the name of Schalcken, revealed the mezzotint mentioned by Edwards. It was subscribed 'Godfrey Schalcken *Pinxt*. William Shipley *Delint*. J. Faber *Fecit*., 1751. Done from the original Painting at Altrop [sic] in the collection of John Spencer Esq.' Since the 'original painting' by Schalcken was found to be still in the collection of Lord Spencer at Althorp House, Northamptonshire,[10] it could be assumed that the version at Maidstone was a copy by Shipley, made when he lived at Northampton in 1751, and brought by him to Maidstone with his other possessions in 1768. Thus one picture by Shipley, albeit unoriginal, exists to illustrate his considerable skill as a painter.

Next to his fame as the Founder of the Society of Arts is his celebrity as the proprietor of a London drawing school. Redgrave in his *Dictionary* confused 'Shipley's School' with the St. Martin's Lane Academy and although Trueman Wood pointed out the distinction between the two institutions,[11] later works of reference have followed Redgrave,[12] and this has made the identification of Shipley's students especially difficult. A list of twenty-one names has been compiled on the basis of statements made by contemporaries, and their performance as candidates for the Society of Arts' premiums has also been checked against the Society's records; a table is given below showing the results of this analysis.[13]

The location of the various premises used by Shipley for his school was established in the course of research into topographical sources for an historical monograph on the houses of the Society of Arts,[14] and a full description of the curriculum of the School was found in the correspondence between Shipley and his pupil Ozias Humphry which is preserved at the Royal Academy.[15] Examining the Humphry mss. at the Royal Academy with the generous assistance of Mr. S. C. Hutchison, the Librarian, proved a fascinating task though it led to a fruitless search for any connection between Shipley and the Academy.

Shipley it is true moved out of London to Maidstone in 1768, the year of the Academy's foundation. But he continued to practise as an artist, as well as undertaking the public work mentioned by J. M. Russell in *The History of Maidstone*, published in 1881, whose brief account of his later life was copied in the *Dictionary of National Biography* and in the two histories of the Society of Arts.[16] With the enthusiastic co-operation of Mr. L. R. A. Grove, Curator of the Maidstone Museum, it has been possible to fill out Russell's sketch from documents in the Museum's collection amongst which are Shipley's own 'memoranda book'—covering the work of the Society of Arts and the Maidstone Society, but particularly precious for the brief personal jottings it contains—and a copy of his previously unknown *Proposal to Establish a Society for Promoting Useful Knowledge in the County of Kent*. This pamphlet, like his other publications, is not to be found in library catalogues and in view of its rarity it has been reprinted below in the documentary appendix.[17] Even Shipley's *Proposals* and *Scheme* for the foundation of the Society of Arts were never preserved in its library; their content is only known because Mortimer printed them in his *Concise Account*, so they will be found republished here in their appropriate place in the narrative of Shipley's life.[18] A large part of Shipley's manuscript correspondence has also been given *in extenso*, either in the narrative or the appendix, so that this book may stand in the place of one which, but for its subject's modesty, might have been long since familiar as 'Shipley's Life, Works, and Letters'.

[b] *The historical setting*

When William Shipley proposed in a brief printed pamphlet an easy method 'to embolden enterprise, to enlarge Science, to refine Art, to improve our Manufactures, and extend our Commerce',[1] he was contributing to a tradition of economic literature which was already a century old in 1753. The promise of a nostrum which would bring strength and riches to the nation had long been the theme of pamphleteers whether respectable political arithmeticians who sincerely believed they knew 'how to pay debts without money', and 'to out-do the Dutch without fighting',[2] or Grub Street writers paid by South Sea, Fishery, and other sectional interests. In beginning the title of his pamphlet with the word 'Proposals', Shipley might well have expected to raise the scepticism of his readers. Between 1701 and 1750 over 250 'Proposals' had been published. There had been 'Proposals for improving the Fisheries', . . . 'for the encouragement of seamen', . . . 'for supplying the nation with money', . . . 'for the due regulation of Servants', . . . 'for employing all the poor', and a host of other apparently desirable objects, few of which had a chance of realisation.[3] Public contempt for the Projector who 'must be delivered by a miracle or starve' as Defoe wrote in his *Essay on Projects*[4] was heightened by the disastrous experiences of the Bubble-year of 1720. Yet there remained those who took comfort in the example of Noah whose building of the ark Defoe called the

6

first project. Malachy Postlethwait reprinted much of Defoe's essay in his great *Universal Dictionary of Trade and Commerce*,[5] which he compiled during the years 1730 to 1755. In noting Shipley's scheme for a Society for the encouragement of Arts, Manufactures and Commerce, he recalled how 'The Great Colbert of France . . . used to declare, That he thought he spent his time well in reading over a hundred proposals for the advancing the wealth and commerce of France, though but one of them deserved to be encouraged. And while other nations are studiously cultivating the arts of commerce, we shall hardly think them undeserving our regard, while our whole dependence is upon them.'[6]

Postlethwait believed that 'commerce should seem to be the original Parent of the Arts and Sciences'[7] and Shipley wished to enlarge commerce through fostering the arts and sciences. However, economic strength was not Shipley's only objective; he wished 'to render Great Britain the school of instruction as it is already the centre of traffic to the greatest part of the known world'.[8] Precedents for his 'Proposals' need not be sought amongst the numerous schemes for improving the national finances, or for discouraging imports and encouraging exports, but amongst the smaller number of plans to foster the inventive talents of the people through the foundation of societies.

The association of private citizens for public purposes is a phenomenon which may be expected to occur in communities which have to some extent petrified their traditional institutions of government. In medieval times religious, local and occupational organisations provided a framework for most human aspirations. Under the absolute monarchies of the sixteenth and seventeenth centuries initiative flowed from the Crown. In England in the eighteenth century, however, the executive government was not only limited constitutionally but was largely preoccupied with the finance and the prosecution of a recurring series of wars. It is in this century that we find emerging organisations for the attainment of national aims which bear the relatively new name of 'societies'. As the fear of religious and political persecution lifted with the end of the seventeenth century, so the desire to form associations grew amongst Englishmen.[9] Coffee-house meetings turned themselves into clubs and many clubs were dignified with the names of societies. 'The Society of Free and Candid Enquiry' was the impressive name adopted by the habitués of 'Robin Hood' tavern in London.[10] Mutual-improvement societies of tradesmen such as the Spitalfields and Manchester Mathematical Societies of 1717 and 1718[11] were matched at the other end of the social scale by the Spalding Gentlemens' Society of 1710[12] and the Dilettanti Society of 1732. The Dilettanti, despite their serious and valuable work for archaeology and art patronage, publicly admitted that 'Friendly and Social Intercourse was undoubtedly the first great object in view'.[13] Their early Minute books contain parodies of the resolution making procedure of more serious bodies which recall seventeenth-century satires on House of Commons arrogance and look forward to the Pickwick Club. Their use of a Roman toga was more innocent than the dress of the Monks of Medmenham, but it may be regarded as part of the same tendency to ritualism, more serious manifestations of which could be found in revived Freemasonry and Rosicrucianism. The 'Society for the encouragement of Learning' which was established in 1735 'to institute a republic of letters for promoting the Arts and Sciences'[14] was probably a masonic lodge and even the Society of Antiquaries had strong ties with Freemasonry.[15]

Although the Society of Antiquaries sometimes claimed an Elizabethan pedigree in the eighteenth century,[16] the senior and most respected English society in Shipley's time was undoubtedly the Royal Society of London for the Promotion of

8

Natural Knowledge. The story of its informal beginnings in the late 1640s as a fulfilment of Bacon's dream of an 'invisible college' is well known.[17] After the Restoration it received Royal patronage and became the centre for the study of experimental science in England. No other national scientific society was to be established in England until Shipley founded the Society of Arts in the middle of the eighteenth century. Shipley's Society succeeded because it complemented the work of the Royal Society and was founded at an opportune moment. H. B. Wheatley, a Victorian scholar who was steeped in the history of both societies, wrote:

> As the condition of England in the middle of the seventeenth century brought about the foundation of the Royal Society and the popular and widely-spread interest in the investigation of science, so the condition of the country in the middle of the eighteenth century brought about the formation of the Society of Arts for the encouragement of the applications of science for the general good. As Dryden, Waller, Evelyn, and the literary coterie of the Restoration period largely supported the Royal Society, so the circle that surrounded Dr. Johnson took a lively interest in the success of the Society of Arts. The lines upon which the Royal Society was founded were not followed by the founders of the Society of Arts. The latter made an entirely new departure and were strictly original in their scheme. Their objects were national, and the members gave their money and their time not for their own private advantage, nor for the increase of their personal knowledge, but in an attempt to raise the productive powers of the nation itself.[18]

Wheatley was incorrect in writing of the 'strict originality' of the Society of Arts. Similar proposals had anticipated Shipley's great idea and in some measure contributed to it. In spite of

their failure they deserve consideration as stages in the
evolution of his achievement.

Early in 1722, less than two years after the bursting of the
South Sea Bubble, a pamphlet appeared under the title of
*Three Letters concerning the Forming of a Society, To be called The
Chamber of Arts, For the Preserving and Improvement of Operative
Knowledge, the Mechanical Arts, Inventions, and Manufactures.* A
detailed 'Essay towards a Constitution for regulating such a
Society' was printed with the proposal,[19] but its essentials
were given in three paragraphs:

> The Business of this SOCIETY may be to enquire into the
> Manner of performing any Thing Curious or Rare in all
> Arts, Trades, and Manufactures, as well Abroad as at Home,
> and to keep a continual Register of the same; to invite
> ingenious Artists and Mechanics, as well Foreigners, as
> others, to apply to them; and to be at the Charge of Pro-
> moting, and Encouraging, or making Trials and Experi-
> ments in any new Invention, Art, or Manufacture; and to
> give particular Rewards to those that invent or contrive any
> New Tool, or Instrument in Husbandry, or Workmanship,
> by which any Trade or Occupation is benefited, and where
> the Property cannot be secur'd to the INVENTOR by a Patent.
>
> And to enable the SOCIETY to answer these great Ends,
> each Member may subscribe to pay a small Sum Annually,
> and make a Donation on Admittance, of such a Sum as their
> different Circumstances and Inclinations will allow of: And
> to reimburse this Charge, in Case of Success in any very
> valuable Invention, they may, by Agreement with the
> Inventor, have a certain Share in the Patent, or other
> Advantage arising from it.

The Consequences of the Success of such a SOCIETY, will be very much for the Benefit of the Publick: Their Registers will contain the Arts and Mysteries of our Trades and Manufactures; nothing of Use can for the Future be lost to Posterity; and every one that has the Liberty of perusing them, may set his Head to work to make Improvements. Their Contributions will be a continual Fund to help and assist Ingenuity, and no useful Undertaking will be lost, either for want of due Trial, or the Incapacity or Obscurity of its Projector. Even by this Means, we may draw from other Nations their Trades and Manufactures, and make our own Country the Retreat and Succour of every peculiar Genius for ARTS and INVENTIONS.[20]

This was a striking anticipation of Shipley's Society of Arts and when rediscovered in the 1760s was said to have been a possible influence leading to its foundation.[21] But even the anonymous advocate of the Chamber of Arts found it necessary to answer the charge that 1722 was 'not a proper time to introduce anything new, when Projects in general are under so much Disreputation, and so many People reduc'd to Misfortunes by playing with them'. He argued in vain that 'our late Losses and Misfortunes might . . . make us more Industrious, more Inquisitive, and more Diligent, by all honest Means, to retrieve the ill State of our affairs'.[22] It required the more confident atmosphere of the middle of the century before 'those of public spirit' would 'pursue the hint given by the sensible author of those letters',[23] and then it would be as much through Shipley's un-projector like candour and persistent personal canvass as through the power of printed argument from himself or other authors. The great flowering of inventive skill and the increased velocity of economic growth which followed the turn of the century and was, indeed, contemporary with Shipley's public career, has been

often described by historians. The causes of these developments are complex, and are still the subject of debate. Two
factors only need be mentioned here: firstly that by the time
Shipley came to publish his 'Proposals' England had enjoyed
her years of Walpolian peace and prosperity, forgetting the
uncertainty of 'South Sea Time' yet retaining her zeal for
commercial preponderance; and secondly that the inventive
idea had been nurtured by English scientists ever since the
foundation of the Royal Society in 1660.

In his *History of the Royal Society*, a book much read in
Shipley's time, Bishop Sprat defined the scope of the Society's
interests:

These two subjects, *God* and the *Soul*, being only forborn:
In all the rest, they wander, at their pleasure. In the frame
of *Men's bodies*, the ways for strong, healthful and long life:
In the *Arts of Men's Hands*, those that either *necessity*, *convenience*, or *delight* have produc'd: In the *works* of *Nature*, their
helps, their varieties, redundancies, and defects: and in
bringing all these to the *uses* of *humane Society*.[24]

Soon after its foundation, the Royal Society had shown an
interest in improved methods of raising sheep and planting
corn, in 'the propagating of fruits and trees', 'the transplanting
of vegetables', the cultivation of silk in North America, the
discovery of dyestuffs and new 'mechanic arts'.[25] These were
all topics which were to interest Shipley and his friends in the
Royal Society when they founded a new society ninety years
afterwards. In the meantime, the 'Royal' had achieved international eminence from the theoretical work of Boyle and
Newton and had become a continuing target for satirical
writers who could see no practical benefits emerging from
abstract science.[26] Literary ridicule of the 'Virtuosi', which was
undertaken by authors of all calibre in the eighteenth century,

reflected the incredulity of the mass of mankind that anyone should waste his time on incomprehensible experiments, and a semi-affectionate acceptance of them as 'characters' whose odd quirks of behaviour caused by absence of mind, gave an added colour to the *Spectator*'s world. The stories which were to be told of Shipley's supposed arrest as 'a spy or Jesuit' because of his extreme taciturnity and of his missed marriage belong to this tradition.[27]

'Sir Nicholas Gimcrack', Shadwell's improbable scientist whom Addison resurrected in the *Tatler*, was said to have been walking in the fields on Midsummer-day 1710, with his wife, when according to her supposed narration: 'he saw a very odd-coloured butterfly just before us. I observed, that he immediately changed colour, like a man that is surprised with a piece of good luck, and telling me that it was what he had looked for above these twelve years, he threw off his coat, and followed it. I lost sight of them both in less than a quarter of an hour; but my husband continued the chase over hedge and ditch till about sunset; at which time, as I was afterwards told, he caught the butterfly, as she rested herself upon a cabbage, near five miles from the place where he first put her up. He was here lifted from the ground by some passengers in a very fainting condition, and brought home to me about midnight. His violent exercise threw him into a fever, which grew upon him by degrees, and at last carried him off.'[28] The legend of Shipley's marriage is remarkably similar, and though it had no historical basis was confidently repeated a hundred years after his death. 'As to Mr. Shipley,' wrote a Maidstone antiquarian in the early 1900s, 'he was . . . a very absent man—after courting a lady a long while (7 years I believe it was) the morning for the marriage in Maidstone Church was appointed —when it arrived the oblivious savant went out in slippers and dressing gown into the garden as often he did—and lo! a butterfly fluttered by towards the Church! and he realised that there ought he to have been—he arrived—but it was too late. The disgusted bridal party had waited and started [and] the lady would not see him but after another such term relented and married they were at last.'[29]

Shipley's chief collaborators in the Royal Society, Stephen Hales and Henry Baker, also suffered from ridicule and satire in spite of their international reputations as scientists.[30] Yet both were occupied with economic improvements as well as with more abstract studies and would have completely rejected Gimcrack's distaste 'for the Practick'.[31] A modern historian of science has pointed out the considerable interest in industrial chemistry which was taken by Fellows of the Royal Society in Shipley's time.[32] There was certainly no lack of desire in the Society to harness scientific knowledge to practical ends, but the constitution of the Society provided only for the publication of such knowledge and allowed for no direct reward to inventors. The Chamber of Arts proposed in 1722 would have remedied the situation by taking 'up things where they are left by the Royal Society'[33] but it was never established. However, some sixteen years later another attempt was made to extend the work of the Society in this direction.

In 1738 'A Proposal for the Encouragement of Arts and Sciences by the Royal Society' was canvassed by a remarkable projector called Philip Peck, under which the Society would have raised a fund of £1,000 to be employed to assist persons producing new and useful inventions.[34] Peck had already written persuasively in favour of the expansion of British fisheries[35] and he later took an interest in the iron industry and in Irish agriculture.[36] Like Shipley he spent his life pursuing schemes for the public good and he suffered similar rebuffs and disappointments. His career was characterised by an admirer as being 'attended with a variety of Accidents, as the soaring you up to a very high Pitch of Fortune, upon the Foundation of Schemes, well laid in the Opinion of your Friends, being they were crown'd with Success. At other times, from equally as good Judgement and Solid Reason, different Undertakings of yours, for want of Power to carry into Execution, have become abortive. And the very same Persons who applauded your Foresight and Prudence at one time, at another, insulted and neglected you under Misfortunes; alledging all your Disappointments and Losses, flow'd from the Consequences of a giddy Head, fill'd with Projects and Castles in the Air, which had only for Foundation, Chimerical Frenzy . . .'[37] Though not a Fellow of the Royal Society, Peck knew its President, Sir Hans Sloane, and was thus able to get his 'Proposal' considered at a meeting of the Council.[38] It was rejected by an equivocally worded resolution, 'that this Society, as a Society, cannot assist in the establishment of such a foundation; nor will they give any interruption to the design of any other Society, which the proposer now seems to be in hopes may be formed thereon'.[39] The Society's records say nothing about the reason for the rejection, but it was probably due to Peck's suggestion that the subscribers to his scheme should share in the profits of successful inventions—which would have turned the Society into a sort of joint-stock company for the exploitation of patents. To Peck there would have seemed nothing strange in this for he was a projector of the classic sort, but it would hardly have appealed to the Council which set a high value on the good name of the Society. When Shipley came to enlist the support of Fellows of the Society for his own proposals in the next decade, he would in no way link them to the Royal Society by name nor include either patents or distributed profits in his scheme.

Shipley's attitude to the exclusive privileges granted by patents of invention—albeit at considerable expense and through cumbersome legal processes—may be deduced from the fact that he was himself never a patentee in spite of his long career as an inventor and from the refusal of his Society of Arts to grant 'premiums' for inventions which had been or were intended to be patented.[40] 'Premiums' or 'Bountys' were the often interchangeable names used for direct rewards carrying no future privileges paid to inventors or the producers of nationally valuable economic products.[41] Such awards were offered under Acts of Parliament by the Board of Longitude (1713) in England, the Linen Board in Ireland (1710) and the Board of Trustees for Manufacture in Scotland (1727).[42] Shipley wished to extend the system by raising a fund from public subscribers. He was anticipated in England by the Anti-Gallican Association, which was founded in 1745 'to promote British Manufactures, to extend the commerce of England, to discourage the introduction of French modes and oppose the importation of French commodities'. It gave a number of premiums for English lace and needlework between 1751 and 1754.[43] Shipley's 'Proposals' echoed to some extent this economic nationalism, but they envisaged a properly organised Society of Arts rather than the militant dining brotherhood which formed the basis of the Anti-Gallicans.

A closer precedent was the Dublin Society for Promoting Husbandry and other useful arts, which in 1740 had adopted the Revd. Dr. Samuel Madden's plan for awarding premiums.[44] Madden was such an enthusiast for premiums that in the manner of the time he gained the word itself as a sobriquet. Shipley arrived at the same views on premiums through independent investigation, but he made use of the example of the Dublin Society when he came to work out the details of his scheme for an English Society of Arts. He did not become acquainted with 'Premium' Madden until after he had successfully established his own Society. In 1757 Madden told Shipley that he had himself tried to establish a premium fund in

England and had sought the patronage of his 'dear and ever honoured Master the late Prince of Wales but I am sorry to say,' Madden continued in a letter to Shipley, 'though the Prince approved it and my zeal, he told me his Finances would not bear such a Burden, which was fitter for his Royal Father's Encouragement (or words to that Effect) than his, and so it dropped neglected'.[45] Unlike his son and grandson George II took little personal interest in anything beyond the purely political and military spheres and Shipley received no Royal support when he established his Society in 1754. By that time Frederick, Prince of Wales,[46] was dead but the Princess Dowager maintained her late husband's 'second court' at Leicester House and her Clerk of the Closet, Dr. Stephen Hales, gave immense assistance to Shipley in his scheme.[47] If no direct Royal patronage was forthcoming it was not long before most of the Ministers of the Crown and the leading statesmen of all parties joined the Society of Arts.[48] A correspondent of Shipley foresaw this in 1754, when he wrote: 'that no truly benevolent or public spirited Briton can hesitate concerning so good a Design. A Design that when carried into Execution will not only unite in one common Band all real Patriots, or as I should then call them the Patrons of the Nation, but will in time, I hope utterly extirpate all Party distinctions, the Bar of Society and Civil Government: for as we might in Charity conclude that the aim of all Partys is the public good; so all Partys must if that be their Principle join in promoting a design so well calculated for that great end.'[49]

Shipley had many links with the talented group of artists which had received encouragement from Frederick, Prince of Wales.[50] The group felt strongly the need for a national academy of arts. In 1749 one of its architect members, John Gwynn, published an 'Essay on Design' which included 'Proposals for Erecting a Public Academy to be Supported by Voluntary Subscription till a Royal Foundation can be obtained' and 'for Educating the British Youth in Drawing'. Gwynn shared Shipley's belief in the value of drawing instruction for all classes. 'There is scarce any Mechanic, let his Employment be ever so simple,' he wrote, 'who may not receive advantage' from it. He pointed out that although the Royal Society was older and better than the French Academy of Sciences, and the Académie Française itself had become degenerate, yet France had in her Academy of Painting and Sculpture an institution which gave her 'Glory and Advantage'. Were such an academy 'imitated and improved upon', London, Gwynn believed, would become 'a Seat of Arts, as it is now of Commerce, inferior to none in the Universe'.[51] Although there was to be no Royal Academy of Arts in England until 1768, Shipley's Society of Arts and Drawing School went a long way towards fulfilling Gwynn's suggestions in 1754.

The growing sense of professional self-sufficiency amongst the London artists of Shipley's time which made them put forward schemes for academies and societies of art also permitted them to make direct contributions to the public welfare. A major object of their interest was Captain Thomas Coram's Hospital for Foundling Children and Hogarth's work for this important charity has often been described.[52] Shipley also took an interest in the hospital[53] but he went much farther than his brother artists and initiated his own schemes for remedying social evils and assisting the unfortunate. He was indeed the only professional artist to earn a place amongst the great names of eighteenth-century philanthropy. 'Thrice happy the country which can boast of a Howard, a Young, a Hawes, a Shipley', wrote Count Leopold Berchtold in 1789.[54] It will be seen that Shipley was active in prison reform, poor relief and life-saving, the specialities of Howard, Young and Hawes, besides his many other 'plans for the public advantage'.[55]

Shipley's life included in its span the surge of English commercial self-confidence which Defoe celebrated and which was to be feared by Napoleon, the spectacular first stage of the Industrial Revolution from the flying shuttle to steam-powered cotton mills, the flowering of English genius in the arts from Hogarth to Turner, and the growth of English philanthropic endeavour from the first county hospitals to Hannah More's 'Age of Benevolence'.[56] In the shaping of these momentous developments Shipley made a contribution which was both distinctive and significant.

2

PRELUDE

'Encouragement is much the same to Arts and Sciences as culture is to Vegetables.'

Shipley's 'Proposals'

---

[i] *Family background and education*

William Shipley was the third son of Jonathan Shipley, a native of Leeds who had settled in London at an early age, and of Martha, the daughter of William Davies of Twyford, in Hampshire. According to the *Dictionary of National Biography*, William Shipley was born in Maidstone in 1714.[1] Trueman Wood disagreed about the place and questioned the date; he believed that William was born in London and that 'the correct date of his birth might be 1715'.[2] His guesses can now almost certainly be confirmed by the baptismal registers of the united parishes of St. Stephen, Walbrook, and St. Benet, Sherehog. The registers show that William, son of Jonathan Shipley and Martha, his wife, was christened on 2nd June 1715. His elder brother, Jonathan, was christened in 1713, and an older William in 1712.[3] This William most probably died in infancy;[4] had he survived he would have become the heir of Twyford instead of his brother Jonathan, so there is no possibility of his being the William Shipley who founded the Society of Arts.

Jonathan Shipley was thirty-nine in 1715. He had earned his Freedom of the City by service in the Company of Leather-

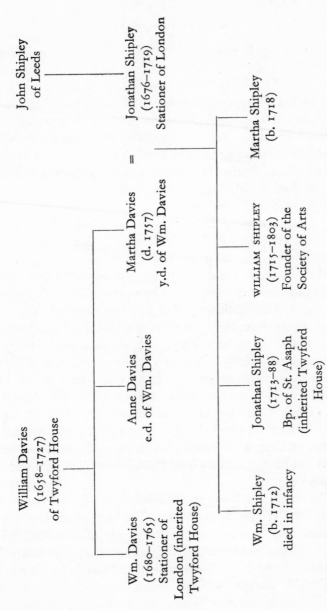

The Shipley and Davies Families

sellers,[5] but was in business as a stationer, and it is as a 'Citizen
and Stationer of London' that he is described on his monument
in Twyford Church.[6] His master in his apprenticeship days had
been Joshua Sharp, a member of the Leathersellers' Company,
whose actual business as distinct from his livery was that of a
stationer and who rose to such distinction in the stationery
trade that he became Sheriff of London and a Knight in 1713.
Sharp trained Jonathan as a stationer, making him and William
Davies, Junior—Martha's brother—his business successors.[7]
The younger William Davies became a member of the
Stationers' Company and although his brother-in-law and
partner never joined it, Jonathan's name is also mentioned in
its records with the designation of a 'Stationer' working in the
'Poultry',[8] which since the latter part of the seventeenth
century had become one of the City's principal centres for the
printing and bookselling trade.[9] Perhaps his sons' taste for
learning grew from early memories of their father's and uncle's
work amidst the authors and printers of Augustan London.

It seems unlikely that Jonathan Shipley was a man of great
wealth for he made no progress in the civic hierarchy and his
London property was far from extensive.[10] Yet his marriage
into a family which linked City to country gentlefolk indicates
that he achieved a certain level of prosperity; by it he provided
for his children a background which would not have been
theirs had his connections been limited to a circle of London
tradespeople.

William Davies lived at Twyford House in the beautiful
Hampshire village of that name. In later years Benjamin
Franklin was to write of the 'sweet air of Twyford' and
County historians have called it 'Queen of Hampshire villages'.
Twyford House was a 'fine mansion' and attached to it was a
comfortable estate.[11] William Davies was evidently well dis-
posed towards Jonathan Shipley, the husband of his younger
and perhaps favourite daughter,[12] and used to entertain him

and his family. Unfortunately, Jonathan died in 1719, during the course of one of his visits to Twyford.[13] The Shipley children then became the responsibility of the Davies family.

The three fatherless children, Jonathan aged six, William aged five, and Martha aged three, probably lived at Twyford House with their mother and grandfather until the latter died in 1727. He bequeathed to each of them £500, to be paid at the age of twenty-one, 'in the meantime their mother to have the interest thereof for their better education and maintenance'.[14] Their uncle, William Davies, Junior, was now master of Twyford, and he took a hand in the upbringing of Jonathan in the following year. The records of the Stationers' Company show that Jonathan Shipley, 'son of Jonathan, late of the Poultry, Stationer deceased', was apprenticed in June 1728 to his uncle William Davies, also of the Poultry and a Stationer.[15] But Jonathan did not persevere with his apprenticeship. In the same year he was sent to Reading School, beginning the formal education which was to lead him to the university and without which his celebrated career in the Church would have been impossible.[16]

William also went to school, but where and when remains unknown. In a communication on education made by him to the Society of Arts in 1782, he wrote of his days as a 'School Boy' when he had expended 'laborious application' on the Latin language which he said he had learnt 'grammatically at school more than nine years'.[17] His name does not appear in the registers of Reading School or of the established London grammar schools of the period. All that can be stated with certainty is that his schooling was sufficient to give him the mental training necessary for the subsequent development of his extensive scientific interests. Presumably at some stage it allowed his talents as an artist to emerge.

For one year at least of his school days, William said that his 'Relations', presumably the Davies family, sent him 'to lodge and board in a house where only the French language was spoken'.[17] He thereby acquired a fluency in French which in later life disposed him to give language teaching by conversation an important place in his ideal system of education. In his 1782 communication he wished the time 'saved to youth in learning languages expeditiously' to be 'employed in learning various Arts . . . which are rarely taught in schools and Academies'. Amongst these he listed astronomy, geography, optics, mechanics, hydrostatics, which were 'Branches of Experimental Philosophy' familiar to him in his early manhood and which had presumably formed part of his own education.

His belief in the value of moral instruction may be either reaction against or the result of his personal experience. He supposed 'that it will be very difficult for any youth who has for a considerable time been educated in a school or Academy, where virtue is carefully taught, to become at once very vicious, almost as difficult for a swan to discharge his snow-white colour and become black'. William's religious beliefs probably derived from his early home life and education. There is no direct evidence available, although his statement that 'it will be no more difficult . . . to learn by heart some selected sentences from the holy Scripture than it is for the youth of Common Schools to learn many thousand verses of the Greek and Latin Poets', sounds like a sentiment based on experience.

William Shipley considered that travel had a great part to play in education. It is known that by his early thirties he was accustomed to making 'tours' into different parts of the country, and that he exercised the method of noting down things of interest which he encountered.[18] In 1782 he urged that parties of young gentlemen should travel about Great Britain and visit places where there were 'phenomena of natural history', important manufactures and trades, well conducted systems of poor relief, and interesting 'Antiquities' such

as 'Abbeys, Roman Roads, Camps, and Barrows', or Gentlemen's seats with 'capital collections' of paintings and sculpture.
To make the most of their travels the youths were to learn
drawing, 'which will be very useful for them to take perspective views of any Machines, Buildings, or Pieces of Antiquities'.[17] Economic development, philanthropic endeavour
and scientific and historical research were to be the lifelong
interests of William Shipley. To pursue these he needed a
means of livelihood, and this he found as a painter and teacher
of drawing, the skill which he believed so valuable in the
education of a gentleman. That he himself acquired it is a fact
relating to his early life about which there can be no dispute,
although the relevant evidence is, regrettably, as meagre in
detail as that relating to his schooling and childhood.

[ii] *Artistic training and the first London period*

'William Shipley, painter, Northampton.'[1] This brief memorandum was made by George Vertue in 1748. It is the earliest
evidence available for Shipley's professional calling, yet he had
almost certainly become an artist some years before his move
to Northampton in 1747. There seems little reason to doubt
the statement made some fifty years later by Edward Edwards
that Shipley 'had been educated in art'. According to Edwards
he was 'said to have been the pupil of a person of the name of
Philips'.[2] It is generally assumed that Edwards referred to
Charles Phillips (1707–47), a successful painter of conversation
pieces and portraits,[3] in which the figures are usually of a small
size. Phillips' dates certainly fit, but otherwise there is no proof
that he took Shipley as his pupil. Shipley probably learned
both figure and landscape painting. He was called a 'landscape
painter' when he was teaching in London after 1754[4] and
before that, in Northampton, he had made his fine copy of
Schalcken's 'Boy blowing a firebrand'.[5] But with only one of

his works surviving and with no details of his professional training available, Shipley is remembered by art historians for his skill as a teacher, not as a practitioner, of art—'for if Shipley did not create masterpieces he made masters instead'.[6]

The success of Shipley's Drawing School in the years 1755–62, which was linked to the progress of the Society of Arts, of which Shipley was celebrated as the founder, probably led writers such as Edwards and Redgrave to ante-date his achievements and to credit him with the foundation of the St. Martin's Lane Academy.[7] This school went back to 1734 and had links with earlier schools dating from the days of Thornhill and Kneller.[8] In the 1750s and '60s it existed side by side with Shipley's school. Pupils passed from one school to the other, and the Society of Arts awarded premiums to pupils from both. The St. Martin's Lane Academy was principally a life school and was used by grown-up artists as well as students. It is not inconceivable that Shipley had himself studied at the St. Martin's Lane Academy at some time between 1734 and 1747, and that having learned to draw and paint he began to teach art, but there is no evidence to support these conclusions.[9]

Trueman Wood wrote that 'there really does not appear to be any satisfactory evidence that Shipley had any Academy in London before 1754'[10] (the date of the Society's foundation) and his words remain valid to this day. But he also dismissed in the same terms the idea that Shipley had lived in London before that year. He seems to have overlooked the interesting memoir of Shipley which was written by Joseph Moser for the *European Magazine* and published in 1803.[11] In it Moser not only testified to Shipley's friendship with his uncle George Michael Moser, a leading figure in the St. Martin's Lane Academy, but to his custom of frequenting Old Slaughter's Coffee-House, an establishment in the same thoroughfare much favoured by the members of the Academy.[12]

According to Joseph Moser, Shipley 'then lodged in Greek Street, Soho'. Moser gives no specific dates, but from a story he tells which will shortly be quoted of 'a disagreeable scrape' in which Shipley was involved at Old Slaughter's during the aftermath of Prince Charles Edward's rising, it can be assumed that he refers to the years 1745 to 1747. As a lodger in Greek Street, Shipley would not have been a ratepayer, but it may not be mere coincidence that a Mrs. Mildmay paid rates as a householder there from 1740 until 1747.[13] There were, of course, many branches of the Mildmay family, yet it seems reasonable to speculate that this Mrs. Mildmay was a connection of the Mildmays of Twyford who were friends and neighbours of the Shipley family,[14] and that it was at her house in Greek Street that he had lodgings during this period.

Another speculation may be made on the basis of Joseph Moser's statement. Greek Street was in the chief foreign quarter of London. Perhaps it was to a house there or elsewhere in Soho that Shipley had been sent to 'lodge and board', where 'only the French language was spoken',[15] when he was a schoolboy, in which case he would have been long accustomed to the society of foreigners. In the anecdote which Joseph Moser recounted he was mistaken for one. But this was not on account of his speech but because of the lack of it.

Joseph Moser wrote:

Some time after the rebellion of 1745 [when there was still a general apprehension of Jacobite intrigues] Shipley's sober appearance and taciturnity had once nearly led him into a disagreeable scrape . . . While the popular opinion ran so strong against Roman Catholic Priests and Jesuits, Mr. Shipley used to frequent Old Slaughter's Coffee-House. He then lodged in Greek Street, Soho, and consequently found it agreeable to take his afternoon tea there, when not

27

otherwise engaged. He seldom spoke, amused himself with the papers &c., laid his sixpence upon the bar and retired. His dress was at this time black, his appearance, as I have observed, solemn, and his taciturnity so remarkable, that it was the opinion of most of the company that 'he did not hold his tongue for nothing'. While conjecture was wearying herself with respect to his character and profession, he innocently administered to her more food for speculation.

It has been stated, that it was the property of his active and energetic mind ever to be studying some plan for the public advantage; consequently he had with him abundance of papers and memorandums. These he used frequently to contemplate at the coffee-house, and, from the idea of the minute, make remarks upon them. The company had been some time wavering in opinion, whether he was a spy in the service of the French Monarch, or a Jesuit delegated by his Holiness the Pope to take care of the concerns of the family of a certain Cardinal;[16] but the production of these papers, some of which might probably contain the ichnography [*sic*] of future manufactures or mathematical diagrams, caused a coalition of sentiments, and it was now on all hands believed that Mr. Shipley, one of the most loyal, benevolent, and inoffensive beings upon earth, was here acting in a double capacity, with a view to remuneration from both these potentates.

In consequence of this suggestion, some of these officious gentlemen soon after intimated to an adjacent Magistrate the danger that might arise to the State from suffering a person of his description to sit for hours together in a public coffee-room without saying a word to anyone; to read, write, and sometimes to draw, unquestionably plans of the dockyards, or charts of the most accessible parts of the channel and coast; at other times, when spoken to, only to answer in mono-syllables; and, in short, do many other things of this nature, contrary to his allegiance, and such as rendered him a very suspicious character.

The Magistrate, who happened to have a greater share of sense and discretion than his informers, instead of sending a warrant, which perhaps the ebullition of the public mind in those times might have justified, desired some of his officers to request the favour of the Gentleman to attend him, which request was instantly complied with. But when Mr. Shipley came to the judgement seat, whether he could not or would not, explain his situation; whether his papers, which might be plans and remarks that probably no one understood but himself, made an unfavourable impression, is uncertain; but it is certain, the Magistrate, who was unacquainted with the hesitative mode of delivery of the culprit, appeared to have considerable doubts of his innocence; and, in fact, matters began to assume a serious appearance when two of his intimate friends, who had heard of the adventure at the coffee-house, came into the room.

'What is the occasion of this crowd?' said one of them.

'We have got a spy and Jesuit in custody.'

'Where is he?'

'There!' was the reply.

'There! Why this gentleman is as loyal a person as any in His Majesty's dominions. He is brother to an eminent Divine of the Church of England.'[17]

'Is this certain?' said the Magistrate.

'Certain!' replied the Gentleman. 'You know me, Sir, and I can vouch for the truth of what I have asserted.'

'Why, then, did he not speak?'

'We know,' continued the Gentleman, 'that it is an offence in certain circumstances, to stand mute at the bar; but this is the first time we ever heard it was any to be *quiet* in a coffee-room. However, as the taciturnity of our friend has involved him in such disagreeable consequences, we will endeavour to prevail with him to be more loquacious in future.'[18]

Joseph Moser does not name the friends of Shipley who helped him out of this predicament. They could have been some of the celebrated artists of the St. Martin's Lane Academy or scientists of distinction.

For if it is probable that Shipley had made friends amongst the leading London artists before he left for Northampton in 1747, it is quite certain that he had been introduced into the chief scientific circle of the metropolis. His friendship with Henry Baker[19] began in this period. Baker practised professionally what in modern times would be called Speech Therapy. He was both successful and prosperous in this work and had sufficient leisure to play a leading part in the deliberations of the Royal and Antiquarian Societies. He had published studies on Natural History and was especially well known for his book on the use of the microscope. When Shipley told him that he was going to live in Northampton, Baker asked to be kept informed of any geological rarities or other 'natural curiosities' which might be discovered in the area. Shipley promised to report on anything of interest. A correspondence was begun which lasted until Shipley returned to London in 1753.

[iii] *The move to Northampton, 1747*

The Northampton to which Shipley moved in 1747 was full of neatly built late seventeenth- and early eighteenth-century houses. Few buildings were of a date earlier than the devastating fire of 1675, and this absence of medieval, Tudor or Jacobean irregularities was pleasing to contemporaries, who thought the town 'as pretty . . . as any in England'.[1] Shipley took lodgings in a street known as The Drapery in the western quarter of the town and not far from the horse market, which was 'reckoned to exceed all others in the kingdom'. The horse fairs proved of great interest to him and helped to confirm his views on 'the good effects of rewards'.[2] Mortimer described how his thinking on this matter developed:

At Northampton there are annually two very considerable fairs for horses, at each of which, several thousands are exposed to sale, and the dealers in horses resort to these fairs to purchase them, not only from different parts of this kingdom but also from foreign countries: Mr. Shipley having observed for some time what large sums of money were annually returned by this branch of trade, was induced to enquire into the cause of the success of these fairs, and was informed that the premiums of the king's plates, and of the plates given by private subscriptions for races in the different counties of the kingdom had encouraged a great number of jockies and other dealers to breed race horses, and for that purpose to import Arabian stallions, by which means in process of time the breed had been so considerably improved, that vast numbers of valuable horses not only proper for races, but also useful in the field of battle, and for many other purposes, had been bred in many counties, and had been sold at much higher prices than were formerly given for the best horses at these fairs; and he was also informed that the value of the exports of horses to foreign parts at this time was computed to amount at least to thirty thousand pounds per annum.

From this remarkable instance of the good effects of the premiums given at horse races, so little known or attended to by the generality, who only look upon these races as seminaries of every species of vice, Mr. Shipley made this sensible reflection: if such is the advantage arising to my country from these partial premiums, which in appearance seemed only calculated to promote a favourite diversion, how glorious, how extensively useful it must prove, to establish public premiums for the general encouragement of Arts, Manufactures and Commerce![2]

Although Shipley earned his living as a painter in Northampton,[3] he devoted much of his leisure time there to his scientific interests. He was fortunate in finding a flourishing philosophical society established in the town. Its most recent historian has described it as 'one of many such societies that have not yet received their full due'.[4] Shipley called it the 'Royal Society in miniature'.[5] Its members aimed at 'improving themselves and each other in natural knowledge'.[6] They listened to papers on magnetism, electricity, mechanics, hydrostatics, pneumatics, optics and meteorology. Shipley attended their meetings first of all as a guest, and seems to have become a member early in 1748. As a friend of Henry Baker, he was certain of a warm welcome. He told Baker in a letter dated 18th October 1747, the first of a series which he wrote to him during his stay in Northampton, that at the meeting of the Society held 'Last Tuesday' (i.e. 13th October), 'some of the Gentlemen, hearing that I had the honour of your Acquaintance asked me if I thought that their correspondence with you would be agreable'. Shipley thereupon undertook to write to Baker, for which he 'received the thanks of the whole Society'.[5] Baker 'willingly embraced' this offer of a correspondence with the Northampton Society. Writing to Shipley on 22nd October he expressed his belief that 'Nothing can promote knowledge and discover Truth as much as a mutual Communication of Observations made by People in the same Enquiries' and went on to promise that 'Whatever therefore you shall be pleased to send me that is either curious in itself or can aid in any Manner to rectify a Mistake or inform of something not so well known without it, I shall if you give me leave communicate in your name to the Royal Society where

I can assure it a candid and kind Reception, and in return I shall willingly transmit to them anything of a like nature as shall be brought by the said Society or come to my knowledge by them'.[7]

Baker's reply was communicated by Shipley to the Society early in November 1747, and one of the leading members, Dr. Philip Doddridge, was deputed to answer it. Doddridge had already achieved a national reputation as a theologian and educationalist but was modest about his attainments as a scientist and about the standing of the Northampton Philosophical Society. He was 'a little surprised' that 'good Mr. Shipley (to whom we are very much obliged) should mention it even as a contingency that we might have an opportunity of communicating anything which might do the least towards enriching your [Baker's] elegant, ample and curious collection'. He warned Baker 'that you are to expect nothing from me as a philosopher', though he offered him his personal friendship and spiritual support.[8] Yet the postscript of his letter, describing a medical phenomenon, was esteemed of such importance by Baker as to warrant its communication to the Royal Society. Baker's warm response expressed his pleasure at the opportunity of winning 'the Esteem and Good Wishes of so benevolent a Mind'.[9] They corresponded regularly during the next three years and frequently exchanged complimentary messages to and from William Shipley. The subjects Doddridge treated in his letters to Baker he also discussed with Shipley, and in one instance Shipley anticipated a favour which Doddridge had asked Baker to perform. Doddridge was interested in cases of telepathy and premonition. Early in 1748 he asked Baker to look up a passage in 'Lord Bacon's works' which he had heard was concerned with these matters. Before Baker could reply, Shipley had supplied the reference, having looked it up during a visit to London.[10]

Shipley had spoken to him enthusiastically about Baker's

seventeen-year-old son, David. Under his father's expert tute-
lage David Baker had developed a talent for science and
languages and had published his first book before he was
fifteen.[11] In discussing the boy's progress, Shipley would have
revealed to Doddridge his interests in education, and Doddridge was, of course, in a favourable position to gratify them.

Doddridge's Academy, 'in many ways the most famous of
Nonconformist seminaries',[12] was in Sheep Street, the northern
continuation of The Drapery. There Shipley was able to par-
ticipate in a community where religious exercises and the study
of divinity were blended with scientific experiments, philanthropic endeavour and social conviviality; and where Churchmen and Sectarians, the 'nobility, Gentry and Others', could
be united by their friendship for its head. No doubt this
encouraging environment assisted Shipley to mature his plans.

While still but a guest of the Northampton Philosophical
Society, Shipley put forward a proposal that the Society should
institute an annual prize medal, which, he told Baker, 'they
seem much to approve . . . and next Tuesday [i.e. 20th October
1747] it is to be put to the vote'. The outcome of the meeting
is not mentioned by Shipley in his subsequent letters to Baker,
and no minutes or reports of the proceedings have so far come
to light. But the suggestion is interesting because it shows that
as early as 1747 Shipley was beginning to think about prizes
and their utility as a method of stimulating inventiveness. This
was probably one of the occasions which Mortimer refers to
when he writes of Shipley having, at Northampton, frequently
taken 'an opportunity of mentioning the good effects rewards
had been productive of, on many public and private occasions'.

According to Mortimer, Shipley quoted 'in support of the
truth of his remark . . . several instances both from ancient and
modern history: but what more particularly engaged [his] . . .
attention to this subject was a familiar instance which then fell
within his own observation'. The 'familiar instance' was the

stimulus given to British horse breeding by the prizes offered
by the King and private subscribers at the races, which as has
been seen attracted Shipley's notice in the Northampton horse
market.

Shipley's acquaintances amongst what Mortimer called the
'learned and ingenious gentlemen of Northampton' agreed
with him about the value of rewards but did not encourage
him in his scheme to form a national Society for their distribution.

> He met [writes Mortimer] with so little encouragement from
> them, owing to the great difficulties which they apprehended
> must necessarily attend the carrying so extensive a scheme
> into execution, that he was totally dissuaded from attempt-
> ing it, and for the present laid aside all thoughts of making
> any further applications on that head, but as he thought the
> proposals might one day prove of some utility, he carefully
> preserved them; and happily, some time after, a favourable
> circumstance once more expanded the wings of expectation,
> and opened a door to a more successful attempt to accom-
> plish this important design.[13]

The 'favourable circumstance' occurred in 1751, when
Shipley successfully overcame the Northampton fuel profiteers.
Before that, however, he co-operated with his friends of the
Northampton Philosophical Society in the less direct method
of enlarging national resources by means of scientific experi-
ment.

[iv] *Scientific curiosity, 1748–50*

Whatever the outcome of his proposal that the Northampton
Philosophical Society should institute a prize medal,[1] it in no
way affected Shipley's enthusiasm for the general work of the

Society. In May 1748 he informed Baker that he was 'now myself a member' and that he was endeavouring to assist the Society in its meteorological observations. He had worked out a method of improving the readings on barometers and sent Baker a description and diagram for his consideration, for he had no doubt that Baker would 'presently perceive whether it is practicable or not' and be able to obtain an estimate of the cost of making the proposed instrument.[2] Shipley's barometer turned out to 'be very troublesome to make' and to have been 'long since published to the world' by Descartes. He had 'accidentally thought of it without the least previous knowledge of Descartes' scheme', and Dr. Doddridge, Charlewood Lawton and others had 'thought it might be put in practice and esteemed it a new contrivance'. This first recorded experiment of Shipley's showed that he was not destined to be an original scientific thinker. His genius was to be revealed in the world of men, and of ideas about human problems, and not in theoretical calculations; yet he understood their value and furthered the cause of science by encouraging and assisting others to undertake experiments.

Baker, who had a profound knowledge of geology, was always grateful for the specimens which Shipley collected for him or arranged for others to collect for him in Northampton-shire and the neighbouring counties. Soon after arriving in Northampton Shipley had obtained for Baker 'a variety of Petrified shells and some Kettering stone'. He mentioned his intention of visiting the mines of Staffordshire, where he would search for fossils.[3] In May 1748 he was still hoping to undertake the trip, and he told Baker that he would 'not fail to enquire amongst the miners for the Fossils'; Charlewood Lawton, who was 'going shortly to live in Derbyshire', would collect fossils for Baker in that county. Baker replied expressing his gratitude and asked to be sent an 'Impression of a Fish in coal' which he thought Shipley had mentioned to him. There is in fact nothing about this in Shipley's letters to Baker, but he may have talked about it to Baker during a visit to London.[4] Two years later, in 1750, Baker was interested to receive from Shipley the impression of 'an unknown production' which Baker believed 'to approach to something of the cones of the fir kind'.[5]

Baker was also glad to accept the specimens of animalcules which Shipley offered to send him. In January 1748/9 Baker wrote to Dr. Doddridge sending his compliments to the Northampton Philosophical Society 'and to Mr. Shipley in particular and pray tell him I take it as a great favour, if he can send me some of the wheel animals'.[6] These 'wheel animals' were Rotifera, a class of animalcule distinguished by the wheel-like motion of their head organs. Baker had shown how the microscope could be used to investigate the various categories of 'wheelers', as he sometimes called them.[7] Doddridge told him that Shipley had 'some dry Mud on which there are Eggs of Wheel Animals which he will send you with some other little things as soon as he conveniently can. He finds pretty good encouragement here'.[8]

Seventeen-fifty was a year of earthquakes in England. The newspapers carried sensational reports of the shocks, and some clergymen saw them as portents of Divine wrath. The scientists were interested in collecting precise information. On 8th February, 'between 12 and 1 o'clock after noon', it was reported, 'an earthquake was felt throughout London and Westminster'.[9] Baker sent an account of it to Doddridge to be communicated to the Northampton Philosophical Society and also enquired 'if you at Northampton felt anything?'.[10] Doddridge replied that he was 'credibly informed that a Lady of this Town, Sister to Mr. Wilmer,[11] our late representative in Parliament, and a Gentleman, son to Dr. Conant,[12] a very celebrated Preacher of the Last age, both of them felt a strange shock just at the time it was felt in London. I am not acquainted with either of them, but I have the report from very good hands, and indeed Mr. Shipley is my immediate author'.[13]

The more violent shock which troubled London on 8th March[14] seems to have left Northampton untouched, for Doddridge could not 'find that anything was felt there'.[15] On 30th September, however, according to the newspapers and magazines, Northampton suffered under a shock of record proportions.[16] Doddridge responded to Baker's request[17] for information by sending an account which was so meticulously detailed that it was published in full in the *Philosophical Transactions* of the Royal Society. 'Some', he wrote, 'thought the Quivering of the Ground continued longer than others apprehended, but I have met with none, that in this respect were so accurate in their Observation, as my ingenious friend Mr. Shipley, who assures me he felt four distinct concussions, the second and third of which were more violent than the first and last, all with 3 or at most 4 seconds.'[18] Shipley was evidently well trained in the assessment of these seismic phenomena.

Shipley was also interested in numismatics. He had a considerable collection of ancient Roman coins and medals. Some were originals and others were sulphur casts made by Baron Phillipe von Stosch, from the great continental collections.[19] Shipley was skilled at making plaster casts from these sulphurs as well as from his originals, and he appears to have undertaken to supply a set to Dr. James Parsons, the celebrated physician and antiquary.[20] In his letter about the barometer Baker told Shipley that 'Dr. Parsons . . . will be very thankful for the Casts you intend him. I should likewise myself be very glad of any you have to spare which you have not favoured me with already, and in particular the Heads of all the Roman Ladies would be highly acceptable'. Shipley replied on 3rd July 1748, promising 'to send the Empresses Heads . . . as soon as I can possibly get them finished'. In fact three years were to elapse before he was able to finish them. By then he had made a set of 100 casts—representing the best of his own collection—and covering the 'Roman Commonwealth' as well as the Empire. He sent them to Baker in a five-drawer cabinet 'stained of a fine red'. 'The Gems being set on a ground of that colour,' Shipley thought, 'gives them a very pretty appearance.'[21] Within the limitations of his moderate means Shipley indulged the tastes common in his period amongst wealthy connoisseurs of art and science. He was also to emulate those of the rich who contributed to charitable endeavour. In this sphere, however, he became more than the follower of a trend of his time; he was to guide men of many classes towards a national objective.

3

ACHIEVEMENT

---

*'Some of the Nobility, Clergy, Gentlemen, and
Merchants, having at heart the Good of their
Country . . .'*

Shipley's Notice *To the Publick* on behalf of the
Society of Arts, 1754

---

[v] The Northampton Fuel Scheme and the 'Proposals', 1751–2

In June 1751 William Shipley apologised to his friend Henry
Baker for delaying his promised present of 'several impressions
of antique Gems' and excused himself on the grounds that he
had 'been very much engaged in a variety of business'.[1]
Amongst the engagements which would have occupied
Shipley at this time were his project for combating the
Northampton fuel profiteers and a renewed canvass of his
'Proposals' for establishing a premium society.

According to Mortimer it was the success of the fuel project
which prompted Shipley 'once more to turn his thoughts to
the revival of his favourite plan for encouraging Arts, etc.'.[2]
Mortimer suggests that the fuel project was initiated in the
summer of 1751 and continued in operation until 1753, yet as
early as 8th July 1751 Shipley was to refer to his 'Proposals'
as having been 'much approved by Gentlemen of Fortune and
Taste'.[3] No doubt the success of the project made for the
success in canvassing the proposals, but the two were contem-
poraneous rather than consecutive operations.

Shipley makes no direct reference to his fuel project in his letter to Baker, and since no other sources appear to be available, Mortimer's well-known account will be quoted in full:

In the year 1751, having observed the oppressive methods made use of by the engrossers of wood and coals in the town of Northampton, whose usual custom was, to lay in great stores of these commodities in summer, and to sell them retail to the poor at very exorbitant prices, during the rigour of the winter, he [Shipley] formed a scheme for preventing this cruel practice in future, by proposing to some of the substantial inhabitants to raise a fund by voluntary subscriptions in order to buy in a stock of fuel on the best terms, and to retail it to the poor at prime cost, subject only to the incidental charges of warehouse room, and a moderate profit to a man to take care of the stock. The persons applied to, not readily agreeing to this proposal, Mr. Shipley, who had this act of charity greatly at heart, resolved to employ what money he could spare in this benevolent plan; and accordingly laid out twenty guineas in purchasing wood and coals; which he determined to sell to the poor at first cost. When those to whom he first imparted his resolution saw that he had actually set the example himself, and had made a beginning, then they concurred with the plan, and subscribed about one hundred and twenty guineas to be employed in this undertaking; and appointed him their treasurer, for two years successively. By means of this subscription, sea coal[4] for which the poor were obliged, in the winter, to pay twenty pence per bushel, was delivered at thirteen pence; pit coal was reduced from two shillings and sixpence to one shilling and five pence; and wood from fourteen, to nine pence per hundred weight.[5]

His fuel project shows that Shipley was a traditionalist as well as an innovator. To supply the poor with coals or wood at cost price had been an object of pious benefactions and municipal government policy since Tudor times.[6] However, contemporary economic thinkers were beginning to doubt the wisdom of any interference with the forces of the market. Josiah Tucker believed that 'the Self-Love and Self-Interest of each Individual will prompt him to seek such Ways of Gain, Trades, and Occupations of Life, as by serving himself, will promote the public Welfare at the same Time',[7] and Adam Smith was to compare 'the popular fear of engrossing and forestalling . . . to the popular terrors and suspicions of witchcraft'.[8] Yet both writers were to advocate the giving of premiums to encourage new arts and manufactures;[9] and this was the essential idea behind Shipley's 'Proposals'.

Mortimer gives the following text:[10]

PROPOSALS

For raising by subscription a fund to be distributed in PREMIUMS for the promoting of improvements in the LIBERAL ARTS and SCIENCES, MANUFACTURES, &c.

As riches are acknowledged to be the strength, Arts and Sciences may justly be esteemed the ornaments of nations. Few kingdoms have ever been formidable without the one, or illustrious without the other; or very considerable without both.—Does it not then behove every nation to cultivate and promote amongst the members of her own community, what are so apparently and eminently conducive to her interest and glory? Encouragement is much the same to Arts and Sciences as culture is to Vegetables: they always advance and flourish in proportion to the rewards they acquire, and the honours they obtain.—The Augustan age amongst the Romans, and some preceding ages amongst the

Greeks, were remarkable for the delicacy of their taste and the nobleness of their productions; they have recommended and endeared themselves to all posterity by many valuable monuments of genius and industry. None, I presume, will imagine that the men of those times were endued with natural abilities superior to the rest of mankind in former ages, or in this our present time, but their abilities, originally equal, rose to this superiority, by falling into a more fertile soil, and being exerted under more favourable influences. Had the same advantages been enjoyed, even in the most supine and barbarous periods, there is no doubt but genius would have shined, and industry toiled, and very probably with equal success.

Profit and honour are two sharp spurs, which quicken invention, and animate application; it is therefore proposed that a scheme be set on foot for giving both these encouragements to the liberal sciences, to the polite arts, and to every useful manufactory. That with this view a fund be raised by subscription for the distribution of some suitable premium or honorary gratification for any and every work of distinguished ingenuity. That whoever shall make the most considerable progress in any branch of beneficial knowledge, or exhibit the most complete performance in any species of mechanic skill, whoever shall contrive, improve, execute, or cause to be executed any scheme or project calculated for the honour, the embellishment, the interest, the comfort (or in time of danger, for the defence of this nation) may receive a reward suitable to the merit of his services. Such an undertaking, it is thought, may easily be established, and as easily supported, by a body of generous and public spirited persons, and it is hoped may prove an effectual means to embolden enterprise, to enlarge Science, to refine Art, to improve our Manufactures, and extend our Commerce; in a word, to render Great Britain the school of instruction, as it is already the centre of traffic to the greatest part of the known world.

Northampton, 8th June 1753

Shipley did not publish these 'Proposals' in a printed form until June 1753, and in the following year their aim was accomplished by the establishment in London of the Society for the Encouragement of Arts, Manufactures and Commerce. Before that, however, he had also published an account of how his intended Society was to function. This was the pamphlet entitled 'A Scheme for putting the Proposals in Execution', which like the 'Proposals' themselves had been taking shape in Shipley's mind for some time before they appeared in print.

[*vi*] The '*Scheme for putting the Proposals in Execution*', *1753*

Seven months after he had published his 'Proposals' from Northampton, Shipley issued his 'Scheme' in printed form from London. Like the 'Proposals' it is quoted by Mortimer in its entirety, and is sufficiently brief to be repeated here:

A Scheme for putting the Proposals in Execution

When there is a sufficient number of Subscribers to put the scheme in execution, it is proposed that they form themselves into a body, by the name of a Society for the Encouragement of Arts, Sciences, and Manufactures in Great Britain, or by such other title as the subscribers shall agree upon.[1]

Ladies as well as gentlemen are invited into this subscription, as there is no reason to imagine they will be behindhand in a generous and sincere regard for the good of their country.

It is also proposed that the subscribers shall chuse from

44

amongst themselves a president, one or two vice-presidents, a treasurer, and a secretary.

All the articles relating to the scheme may be settled by balloting, and each subscriber shall be intitled to as many votes as are in proportion to his subscription.[2]

The premiums may be honorary and pecuniary, and adjudged in the following manner. Some time before the date fixed for that purpose, the specimens may be sent by the candidates without any name, to the secretary, who may give receipts for them, and mark each particular receipt and specimen with the same number.

At the time agreed upon for adjudging the premiums, a committee being chosen, and some of the ablest judges of each particular Art, Science, or Manufacture, called in to their assistance, the performance of the several candidates may be examined, and their superior merits determined; then the persons who produce the receipts, whose numbers correspond with those of the best specimens, may afterwards claim the prizes. If a profound secrecy is previously enjoined to the competitors, in all cases that will admit of it, under the penalty of being for ever excluded the benefit of the premiums, it is thought there can be no room for prejudice or partiality.

In particular cases, as for very curious and valuable inventions or improvements, &c. gold-medals may be given (which may serve both for premiums and also for honorary gratifications) of such value, and with such devices, as shall be thought proper by the subscribers; but for common inventions or improvements, pecuniary premiums are judged sufficient.

There may be given with the medals, certificates signed by the president, vice-president, treasurer, and some of the principal subscribers, signifying what honours the acquirers have been intitled to, and what rewards they have obtained;

therefore if a medal be got by a person, whose circumstances may oblige him to part with it, yet still a certificate will perpetuate the honour he has received.

Certificates may likewise be given with the pecuniary premiums, which will be of equal use.

If considerable premiums were given to the inventors, and still greater to the improvers, if thought worthy, and the greatest of all to those who shall most amply execute or cause to be executed, the said inventions or improvements, it may be presumed this would be attended with beneficial consequences.

Should the subscriptions not be sufficient at first for so many premiums as might be wish'd; a beginning may be made with giving rewards for the following articles, or some others that may be judged of the most important to the nation, viz.

For improvements in the present plans of education, in naval affairs, in husbandry, and particularly for the introducing of such Manufactures as may employ great numbers of the poor, which seems the only way of lessening the swarms of thieves and beggars throughout the kingdom, and relieving parishes from the burden they labour under, in maintaining their numerous poor, as well as rendering multitudes of the unemployed lower class of people useful to the community and happy in themselves.

Premiums may also be given for the revival and advancement of those Arts and Sciences which are at a low ebb amongst us; as Poetry, Painting, Tapestry, Architecture, &c. As above all other people the English are endued with talents peculiar for improvements in Arts and Manufactures, so by their most extensive commerce, they will of course reap greater advantages from such improvements, when made, than any other nation whatever.

London, 7th December 1753[3]

Shipley had been working on his 'Scheme' since at least 1751, when Henry Baker had offered 'to oblige' him 'with materials from the Dublin Society'[4] and had advised him to seek the assistance of Dr. Stephen Hales. No correspondence between Shipley and Baker has survived for the period from July 1751 to August 1753. But it is known that they had several discussions during Shipley's visits to London in 1752 and 1753, and that Baker told Shipley that he shared his belief in the benefits which would arise in England of a 'Society to give premiums in the manner of one in Ireland', although he 'doubted the possibility of bringing it into effect'.[5] Yet, in recommending him to approach Dr. Hales, he was, as has been indicated in a previous study, putting Shipley in touch with the influential patrons who would make his idea a reality in 1754;[6] by supplying him with information about the Dublin Society he was showing him how successful a premium-giving organisation could become.

The 'Dublin Society for Promoting Husbandry and other useful arts' had been founded by voluntary subscribers in 1731. In 1740 it had adopted a plan for awarding premiums put forward by the Rev. Dr. Samuel Madden, which foreshadowed

The seal of the Dublin Society for Promoting Husbandry and other useful arts

Shipley's 'Proposals'.[7] Madden wrote: 'Let a proper Emulation be raised, let due Countenance and Rewards be once assigned to all who thus labour for their own honour and public good, and I make no doubt, but our land will be as famous for producing new Inventions, as for being free of Serpents and Toads.'[8]

By 1753 the Dublin Society could afford to offer premiums with an annual value of £852, to which Dr. Madden himself promised a further £231. Baker probably sent Shipley one of the printed lists of 'Premiums promised by the Dublin Society [and] by Dr. Madden'. In his 'Scheme' Shipley advocated the offer of premiums for the same general categories—husbandry, manufactures, and arts—as were employed by the Dublin Society, and he specifically mentioned one of Dr. Madden's premium subjects—the tapestry industry—as being in need of encouragement. Both Madden and the Dublin Society offered premiums to young painters, which was no doubt the method Shipley had in mind when he wrote of 'advancing' the art of painting. It was, in any case, to be adopted by his Society immediately on its foundation.

Yet there were certain differences between Shipley's scheme and the Dublin Society of 1753. Unlike the Dublin Society at this date, Shipley provided for the inclusion of women in his Society and for the award of medals as honorary premiums.[9] The London Society of Arts was to be a pioneer in both respects. Four of his objects for special encouragement—Naval Affairs, Education, Architecture and Poetry—did not figure in the Dublin Society's premium lists at this date.[10] All but the last were to be the work of the London Society, and Shipley probably included them in his scheme through personal preference and the influence of his friends in England. He would have had opportunities of meeting with poets and architects in his London days, though there is no direct evidence to connect him with practitioners of either art. The

Gods. Schalcken Pinx: W.m. Shipley Delin.t.   J. Faber fecit 1751.

Mezzotint of *A Boy Blowing a Firebrand* from a painting by Shipley after Schalcken.

Twyford House, Hants.
Shipley's childhood home.
Photograph of the west front.

Craig's Court, Charing Cross.
Shipley's first London house
was No. 8 on the left of the
photograph.

Knightrider House, Maidstone.
Probably Shipley's last home.

inclusion of Education reflected a lifelong interest and may also point to the influence of Dr. Doddridge; there is no doubt that 'naval affairs' owe their inclusion to a suggestion from Dr. Hales.

It may be recalled that Shipley had written to Baker from Northampton in July 1751 to say that his 'Proposals' were 'much approved by Gentlemen of Fortune and taste'.[11] According to Mortimer, he also took advice about his 'Scheme' from persons living in the Northampton area. These were the Earl of Halifax, President of the Board of Trade, whose seat was at Horton, and some unnamed 'ingenious and public spirited gentlemen in the neighbourhood',[12] who may well have included Dr. Doddridge and other members of the Northampton Philosophical Society. It was probably through Dr. Doddridge that he obtained an interview with Lord Halifax, but Doddridge died in Lisbon on 26th October 1751, and Shipley was deprived of a friend who might have given him powerful support for his 'Scheme'. However, as Mortimer put it, 'He also had a recommendation to the Reverend Dr. Stephen Hales of Teddington'.[13]

Dr. Hales knew Lord Halifax and he had another Northamptonshire acquaintance who would most likely have been familiar with Shipley's plans. This was Thomas Yeoman, the millwright who manufactured Hales's ventilators, and who was one of the most active members of the Northampton Philosophical Society.[14] Hales was also well known to Henry Baker. Clearly there were a number of links between Shipley's circle and Hales's, which helped to bring the two together; these links were to be strengthened by correspondence and personal contact between the principals.

For many years Hales had been advocating the public adoption of various inventions which he believed would be of national or humanitarian advantage. Shipley had heard that he 'particularly recommend[ed] Naval Improvements', and had told Baker in 1751 that the proposed Society might begin by offering premiums for inventions of this kind. In August 1753 he wrote to Baker saying that he had received two letters from Hales giving him 'the greatest encouragement to proceed' with his plans. Hales had shown the 'Proposals' to 'many of our Nobility and from their general approbation of them, he thinks it very probable that a scheme for putting them into execution may take place next winter'. But he had advised Shipley 'not to print the scheme as yet, lest the Gentlemen to whom it was shown might forget it by the time that they came to London'.[15] Shipley followed this advice and did not publish his scheme until 7th December, by which time he had left Northampton 'to reside in London' (as Mortimer puts it) 'that he might have the better opportunity of attending the progress of his laudable endeavours for the service of his country'.[16]

With his small financial resources, Shipley took a momentous step in moving to London. For he received no payment for the time and labour he exerted on his project and he could not be certain that the Society he would found would ever be able to pay him or that his future drawing school would prosper as it did. The 'Journey into Hampshire' which he had made in July, and which included visits to Stonehenge and Avebury reported at length in his letter to Baker,[15] may well have had as its principal object a visit to his family at Twyford, to seek advice on his London venture. Certainly he was now preparing himself to face the hazards of the metropolis.

[vii] *The return to London and the foundation of the Society of Arts, 1753–5*

In 1753 the scene of Shipley's life and endeavours became once more the capital of the kingdom. From the end of that year until early in 1755 he lodged with Husband Messiter, the surgeon, in Great Pulteney Street.[1] There he was conveniently placed between the fashionable area surrounding Piccadilly, where many potential subscribers to his scheme had their town houses, and the Strand and Fleet Street area where the initial meetings of his Society were to be held and where lived Henry Baker and other leading members of the Royal and Antiquarian Societies.[2] Nicholas Crisp, the public-spirited jeweller and pottery manufacturer, who Mortimer says was the only other person besides Messiter and Baker known to Shipley in London as 'capable of forwarding'[3] the projected Society, was a little farther away, being a resident of Cheapside. Dr. Hales lived out at Teddington but had lodgings for occasional use in Duke's Court, Westminster.[4]

Messiter, Baker, Crisp and Dr. Hales were to be four of the ten persons who were to attend the first meeting of Shipley's Society, and among the other six were to be two noblemen of wealth, Lords Folkestone and Romney, whose credit would be pledged in support of the project. Dr. Hales was related to Lord Romney, and Lord Romney's sister was the wife of Viscount Folkestone. These connections marked the start of Shipley's canvass in December 1753. Hales had told him that the two peers 'had expressed to him an ardent desire of seeing some such plan carried into execution, and had promised if any such should take place, that they would become subscribers thereto'.[5] Shipley began with Lord Romney, whose town house was at No. 7 Clifford Street,[6] an easy walk from Husband Messiter's; Mortimer continues his narrative:[7]

. . . he waited on Lord Romney to whom his proposals had been communicated by Doctor Hales. His Lordship greatly encouraged him to proceed in his undertaking, and to endeavour to make interest to establish it. Mr. Shipley decently declined it, observing that Doctor Hales had informed him, that his lordship in conjunction with Lord Folkestone, had some such scheme of their own in view, and that he was afraid the setting his on foot might interfere with their lordships' intentions. Lord Romney on this desired Mr. Shipley to proceed on his own, and thereupon signed a paper, of which the following is an exact copy.

'We whose names are annexed, having perused Mr. Shipley's scheme for promoting improvements in Arts and Sciences, Manufactures, &c. in this nation, do much approve of the design, and think that the putting some such plan in execution, will produce effects very beneficial to this nation. We therefore hereby encourage him to apply to the nobility and gentry for the promises of their subscription and interest, to promote and establish some such plan, and as soon as a number of gentlemen and ladies sufficient to make a beginning, have signified their intention of subscribing to such an undertaking, notice will be given of a meeting (the time and place being first agreed on by a majority of the intended subscribers) to consult on proper measures for putting in execution a plan of this kind, and for laying down such rules for the regulation and advancement of it, as shall be judged most conducive to render it useful and extensive to this nation, and satisfactory to all the subscribers. ROMNEY.'

Lord Folkestone, writes Mortimer, 'was not then in town', but when Shipley 'waited on him a few days after', presumably at his town house which was also in Clifford Street,[8] he 'received him very kindly and signified'

. . . his approbation of his scheme, by signing the foregoing paper, and by allowing him to make use of his name to several of the nobility, and at the same time to give him instructions how to proceed.

Thus encouraged, Mr. Shipley considered that unless he made the best use of his time, as the Parliament was to rise early on account of the ensuing general election,[9] his scheme might fail this year, and afterward be regarded as a stale proposal, and therefore he incessantly applied for subscriptions, and after about three months' solicitations got access to thirty-five of the nobility, and to a greater number of other persons of rank.

Mortimer does not give dates for Shipley's meetings with Lords Romney and Folkestone, so that it is not possible to establish exactly when this energetic canvass was initiated. It must have begun after the 7th December 1753, when the *Scheme* was published, and have ended before the 22nd March 1754, when the first meeting of the Society was held. These dates would certainly fit in with Mortimer's estimate of 'about three months', and there is no reason to doubt what he says of Shipley's sense of urgency about his scheme. It must have been a great test of his patience and endurance to wait unheeded in 'outward rooms'[10] and to be repulsed at so many doorways.

The results of Shipley's efforts were far from encouraging. Mortimer says 'that of thirty-five nobles, and a great number of the gentry to whom he had been admitted only fifteen had promised their subscription', and that he had only obtained one more signature to Lord Romney's declaration of support.

Fortunately, this extra signature belonged to a powerful supporter of public improvements. Isaac Maddox, Bishop of Worcester, was Dr. Hales's colleague on the governing body of the Middlesex County Hospital. He had known Dr. Doddridge and had once written to him of the need for some national scheme for social regeneration.[11] When he heard of the poor response to Shipley's plan he, with Lord Folkestone and Lord Romney, urged 'Mr. Shipley to get a few Gentlemen of his Acquaintance to contribute in Order to make a beginning, which Mr. Shipley had said he believed he could do if their Lordships would be so good as to give them a Meeting'.[12] Thus was arranged the first meeting of the Society of Arts. Dr. Maddox (although paying his subscription) was unable to be present, but Lord Folkestone and Lord Romney both attended at Rawthmell's Coffee-House in Henrietta Street, Covent Garden, on 22nd March 1754, 'where Mr. Shipley brought the following gentlemen to consult with their Lordships . . . viz. the Rev. Dr. Stephen Hales, F.R.S.; John Goodchild, Esq.; Mr. Henry Baker, F.R.S.; Mr. Nicholas Crispe (*sic*); Mr. Charles Lawrence; Mr. Gustavus Brander, F.R.S.; Mr. James Short, F.R.S., and Mr. Messiter'.[13]

It may be recalled that Shipley already knew Baker, Crisp and Messiter when he first came to London in 1753. Gustavus Brander and James Short would have known Henry Baker and Dr. Hales through the Fellowship of the Royal Society, and Brander and Baker were also linked as Fellows of the Society of Antiquaries. Little is known of Charles Lawrence except that in 1759 he stood surety for a bond issued by Shipley.[14] He was probably one of Shipley's personal acquaintances. John Goodchild, who was to be elected the Society's first Treasurer, was well known to Dr. Hales as his neighbour at Teddington and as the father of his curate. He was a prosperous linen draper and both his trading experience and his wealth qualified him admirably for the office he was to hold.[15]

A nucleus of ten members had been formed, and during the course of the year the new Society began to put Shipley's long-cherished plan into practice. The authors of the Bicentenary History pointed out that 'the Society's minute-book makes it quite clear that the Society immediately set to work on the basis established by Shipley—the double plan being to use premiums as a means of encouragement and to raise a public fund to provide the premiums'.[16]

The minutes also show that although Shipley acted as Secretary of the Society—taking a note in his own hand of at least eight of the first fifteen meetings,[17] gathering information for its use from the records of the Custom House, buying stationery, arranging accommodation, writing letters on its behalf—he did not dominate its proceedings. The foundation members acted as a team. Their attendance record is displayed chronologically in the table. Shipley leads with a total of 13 attendances out of 15. Next comes Messiter with 12, followed by Goodchild with 10 and Crisp with 9. Lord Romney had 8 and Baker 7, Lord Folkestone 5, James Short 3, and the Bishop of Worcester, Dr. Hales and Gustavus Brander each had 2. Charles Lawrence seems only to have attended at the first meeting.

Members' Attendances at First Fifteen Meetings of The Society of Arts, 22nd March 1754 to 5th February 1755

	22 March	29 March	10 April	24 April	22 May	19 June	17 July	11 Sept.	9 Oct.	27 Nov.	18 Dec.	10 Jan.	15 Jan.	29 Jan.	5 Feb.	Total
Henry Baker	×	×	×		×				×		×				×	7
Gustavus Brander	×	×														2
Nicholas Crisp	×	×		×	×				×		×	×	×	×		9
Lord Folkestone	×	×										×	×	×		5
John Goodchild	×	×		×			×		×	×	×	×	×	×		10
Stephen Hales	×	×														2
Husband Messiter	×	×	×	×	×	×			×	×	×	×	×	×		12
Lord Romney	×	×								×	×	×	×	×	×	8
WILLIAM SHIPLEY	×	×	×	×		×	×	×	×	×	×	×		×	×	13
James Short	×	×	×													3
James Theobald										×		×	×	×		4
Charles Lawrence	×															1
Charles Whitworth											×	×	×	×		4
Bishop of Worcester			×												×	2

Thus Shipley only missed two of these first fifteen meetings of his Society. His attendance is not recorded on 22nd May 1754, nor on 15th January 1755. The first absence may be explained by the weather. Only Baker and Messiter appeared at the meeting and 'the evening being very wet and no more company . . . expected; after waiting about half an hour they broke up without proceeding to business'. The reason for Shipley's second absence, if it in fact occurred, may have been his wish not to appear obviously involved in the judging of the Society's first drawing competition, in which many of the candidates were his own pupils. Rough minutes of the meeting exist in Shipley's own handwriting, but they omit his name. He probably left it out of the list of those present, which included seven members of the Society and four artists, because of a tactful desire to keep the business of the Society separate from that of his Drawing School. This consideration will be discussed in a later section.

The Society of Arts held no meetings between 17th July and 11th September 1754. On the latter date Shipley may well have had qualms about the success of his enterprise. The minutes record that 'as the subscribers were most of them in the Country', Mr. Shipley, 'after waiting about two hours went away without proceeding to Business'. At the next meeting, on 9th October, five members attended besides Shipley and consideration was given to letters received during the vacation. It was decided to delay replying to two inventors who had sent in accounts of mechanical improvements until 'the rest of the Subscribers come to Town'. On 27th November, Lord Romney presided over a small meeting of Goodchild, Messiter and Shipley. Arrangements were made for judging the drawings which had been received in response to the Society's offer of Premiums, and Shipley himself displayed an invention of his own contriving to the Society.[18] Two important new members, Charles Whitworth, M.P., and James Theobald, F.R.S., F.S.A.,[19] attended the next meeting, which was on 18th December, and Henry Baker delivered in a 'Plan' for the government of the Society, suggesting that 'for the orderly Dispatch of Business . . . there be one President, four Vice-Presidents, a Treasurer and a Secretary; to be elected by Ballot . . . annually'. Baker's suggestion was carried into effect on 5th February 1755, the fourth meeting held by the Society in the new year and the fifteenth since its foundation.

Mortimer gives this account of the occasion:[20]

. . . the Society having formed themselves into a body by the title of the Society for the encouragement of Arts, Manufactures and Commerce, proceeded by ballot to the election of their several officers for the ensuing year, when the following noblemen and gentlemen were chosen, viz.

PRESIDENT

The Right Honourable Jacob Lord Viscount Folkestone

VICE-PRESIDENTS

The Right Honourable Lord Romney
The Reverend Dr. Stephen Hales
Charles Whitworth, Esq., and
James Theobald, Esq.,

John Goodchild, Esq., Treasurer; and Mr. William Shipley, Secretary; who was likewise elected a perpetual member, and excused all payments in consideration of his having framed the original proposals and plan for forming this Society, and of the great trouble and fatigue he had undergone in soliciting the encouragement of the nobility and gentry for many months; the same honor was likewise conferred on Mr. Henry Baker, for drawing up a practical plan for carrying Mr. Shipley's design into execution.

Shipley's Society was now set on its long career of public action, destined, as he would have hoped, to outlast the life of its founder, yet to remain the object of so many of his endeavours during the first half-century of its existence.

4

CONSOLIDATION

---

*'It is true in Great Britain so many Improvements have
been already made that some have thought a Scheme
of this kind is here quite needless, but we find that here
is still a Boundless Field for Improvements, in many
Arts, Manufactures and other Articles. . . .'*

Shipley to Franklin, 1755

[viii] Correspondence with Charles Whitworth, 1755

One of William Shipley's principal duties as Secretary of the
Society of Arts was to write letters on its behalf. Since these
were sent to correspondents throughout the country and in
America, they have not, of course, been preserved in the
Society's archives, though their substance may be gathered
from the Society's minutes. Occasionally the Society itself laid
down the phraseology which Shipley was to employ or com-
missioned Henry Baker to give him assistance.[1] However, in
addition to this official and somewhat impersonal correspondence, Shipley wrote a number of letters about the proceedings
of the Society to the President and Vice-Presidents during
their absence from London in the summer of 1755.[2] One of
the Vice-Presidents, Charles Whitworth, returned the letters he
received to the Society and they have been preserved together
with his own letters to Shipley. Whitworth was a well-con-
nected and ambitious Member of Parliament[3] who took a great
interest in the early development of the Society. He responded

promptly to Shipley's reports of its proceedings with comments and suggestions of his own. Shipley was glad to have the support of such a prominent figure when the survival of his institution was in doubt, though he was not always in agreement with his correspondent. His letters to Whitworth display his customary humility, and deference to opinions which conflicted with his own, but they also show how hard and successfully he worked (behind the scenes) to extend the Society's influence to the North American colonies and to the provinces of the mother country.

The earliest surviving letter from Shipley to Whitworth is dated 24th June 1755. It is a short note accompanied by an abstract from part of the minutes of a meeting held by the Society on 8th June.[4] 'The other Part [wrote Shipley] will consist of Abstracts from Letters which were read, the chief of which was from my old Friend Dr. Alexander Garden[5] of South Carolina in which are mentioned all the most material articles in that Province, where there seems to be most room to advance them by Premiums, a copy of which Letter shall shortly be sent.'[6] The reference to Garden by Shipley as 'my old friend' is interesting. Garden had been in North America since 1752. Presumably he had become acquainted with Shipley before that date and it is possible that Shipley had maintained a correspondence with the botanist in the years preceding the foundation of the Society. It seems certain, in the light of this

Shipley's signature in 1755

reference, that Shipley had taken the initiative in proposing Garden as the first Colonial Corresponding Member of the Society on 19th March 1755.[7]

Shipley sent Whitworth a copy of Garden's four-page letter on 15th July. He hoped that it would be acceptable 'to a Gentleman of your Public Spirit'.[8] Seven days later he sent him the minutes of a meeting which contained 'so little News of our affairs I am afraid you will hardly think it worth your perusal'. He concluded this letter by asking a favour which Whitworth as a Member of Parliament had it in his power to grant:

As my stock of Franks is quite exhausted, I have taken the liberty to send you a small Parcel of Letter Covers and beg the Favour that you will frank them for the use of our Society, please to direct them to me in Craig's Court, you will much oblige,

Sir,

Your most obedient servant,

WILLIAM SHIPLEY[9]

Whitworth had 'been from home sometime upon a visit', so he did not reply until 31st July. He 'entirely agreed with [Dr. Garden] . . . that many articles may be produced in our colonies beneficial to them as well as Great Britain and dare say we may procure from their Climate and Situation what we have from China, Italy and Spain, I mean as to Wine, Silk, Cochineal etc. which would enable us to trade with our own people to Mutual Advantage and to contain Balance in Coin with the rest of the world'. He hoped, on Shipley's recommendation, 'to trouble' Garden with 'his thoughts':

As I write this a private letter to you, you will only make

my compliments out of it to the Gentlemen [of the Society],
I have the pleasure to be known to, And believe

Your Friend and Humble Servant,

C. WHITWORTH[10]

On 7th August Shipley wrote a short enthusiastic letter about 'the Addition to our Society of the Reverend Mr. Tucker of Bristol',[11] but on the same day he was himself being addressed on a matter which would introduce a note of controversy into his correspondence with Whitworth. The author of the letter written to Shipley was Charles Powell, the influential Welsh philanthropist.[12] Powell had joined the Society of Arts soon after its foundation and had then obtained advice from Shipley which assisted him in establishing an agricultural Society in Brecknockshire in the spring of 1755.[13] Shipley had sent him the rules and orders of the Northampton Philosophical Society and other 'Hints as were of some service'.[14] On 7th August 1755 Powell sent Shipley news of the progress of the Brecknockshire Society and expounded the benefits which would arise if similar societies were formed in other countries. He hoped some 'Ingenious Gentleman of our Society in London . . . would consider of and improve this Hint'.[15] Shipley made an abstract of the letter and sent it to Charles Whitworth on the 14th. His accompanying remarks show his own enthusiasm for Powell's proposals:

I make no doubt but you will much approve of his Proceedings and Proposals for they will correspond exactly with your Proposals for our corresponding with most of the Counties of this Kingdom.

I believe, Sir, if County Societies were formed according to Mr. Powell's Plan and our Society had such a Correspondence as he mentions that there would be such a Circulation

61

of Useful Knowledge throughout this Kingdom as would exceed our warmest Expectations.[16]

Whitworth replied on the next day in a letter which expressed approval of Powell's plan, but urged its modification. He wondered 'whether the same plan might not be more effectually carried on by its being All connected together under our General Head . . . and be Branches therefrom instead of Separate Societies for the same purpose'.[17]

Shipley communicated both Powell's and Whitworth's letters to a meeting of the Society on 20th August. The Society voted its 'thanks' to both correspondents, but decided to request Powell's permission to print his proposals and to postpone consideration of Whitworth's amendments.[18] Shipley wrote to Whitworth on the 20th describing the debate in the Society on the relative advantages of more county societies or county branches of the London Society (Whitworth's own suggestion) and giving his own opinion on the matter at some length:

I well know, Sir, that you will readily listen to any Sentiments on Public-Spirited Proceedings, therefore I take the Liberty to express my thoughts freely on the late Establishment of the Brecknockshire Society, which plan will I believe if well modelled and carried regularly into Execution be a means of producing things of the greatest Public Utility, for it will then be copied by many Counties, as was the case of the late Reverend Dr. Clarke's Plan for a County hospital and carried into Execution in the City of Winchester.[19] And I think it not at all improbable that the same Spirit of Benevolence may prevail in different Counties in establishing of Premium Societies, and I believe that if such County Premium Societies were established they would more narrowly consider articles proper to be promoted by Premiums in their own Counties than select Clubs of Gentlemen who were only Branches of a National Society.

I believe, Sir, in County Premium Societies there would be no Room for one grand Obstacle to Publick Spirit. I mean a suspicion of Partiality from other such Clubs or Societies which would be, I am afraid, so often the case if there was but one Premium Society and many Clubs of Gentlemen in different Parts of the Kingdom who were only Branches of it: for I believe many Members of such clubs would be partial in the Merits of their own County and think that a share of the Fund was not given to their Countrymen proportionable to their Merits, and therefore they would on that Account withdraw their Subscriptions. Whereas did County Societies distribute their Rewards never so improperly yet still there would be no room for any Umbrage from the Members of Premium Societies in other Counties. And I believe, Sir, that by means of a correspondence of [the] Premium Society[20] with county Societies, your Plan for our Procuring Intelligence of the state of every County in this Kingdom in regard to its Situation, Commerce, Manufactures &c, would be most effectually executed.

I also think that if a considerable number of Premium Societies were established, the Subscription to our National Society would soon be greatly increased for in all probability Benevolence and Public Spirit would soon become very general, and the Promoters of such Societies would reflect that if they had been instrumental in effecting so many considerable things within the narrow Limits of a single County that they might be of much more Public Utility in forwarding a Design the benign Influences of which might not only be extended to the farthest Extremities of this Kingdom but also to the Utmost Limits of our most distant Provinces. In what I am mistaken in these my Conjectures I know that your Candour will excuse me, particularly as they are mentioned with a view of promoting our Affairs.

As I am ordered by the Gentlemen of our Society to write to Mr. Powell, I will at the same time, if with your Approbation, communicate the Substance of your own last letter, but I shall take no such Liberty without your Particular Orders. I am (wishing all possible Success to our Affairs) with great Respect

Sir,

Your most humble,

and most obedient Servant,

WILLIAM SHIPLEY[21]

Whitworth, however, retained his misgivings about Powell's scheme and he reiterated them in a formal letter to the Society on 1st September,[22] which he sent accompanied by a private letter to Shipley. He told Shipley how glad he was to have his private thoughts and that he agreed 'that County meetings are very necessary for the management of our Business in their particular districts. But,' he continued, 'I only argue that they may be more advantageously carried as Branches and Appendages to us, than separate and distinct, dolling away small sums which in an Aggregate fund might be of consequence . . . As to the instance of County Hospitals, they plainly are much better local, from the difficulty of removing the particular Objects; and in every respect greatly different from a Premium Society to encourage Manufactures without respect to Persons and Places.'[23]

As Secretary of the Society, Shipley had to take up a neutral position in what the minutes of the meeting held on 3rd September called 'this nice affair'. He replied to Whitworth, apparently agreeing with his arguments but in fact sheltering behind the corporate will of the Society:

64

Henry Baker, F.R.S., F.S.A. Engraving by
W. Nutter after Thomson.

The Rev. Dr. Stephen Hales, F.R.S.
Engraving by Hopwood after Hudson.

Robert Marsham, 2nd Baron Romney.
Portrait by Sir Joshua Reynolds in the Lecture Hall of the
Royal Society of Arts.

I am obliged by the Favour of yours which was read at our last Meeting amongst other Letters. Several of the Gentlemen were by the force of your Arguments induced to change their Sentiments in regard to Mr. Powell's Proposals for County Premium Societies but others amongst them retained their first Opinions of the matter and thought that if County Societies for Premiums were established in many Places many beneficial Effects would by such Means be produced to this Kingdom. After several debates concerning the Affair Mr. Powell's Letter was ordered to be read again and every particular Circumstance of it reconsidered. Which being done they thought that as Mr. Powell had been writ to for leave to print this letter that if he complied with their request they were afraid they could not genteely excuse themselves from publishing it: but they agreed that the affair be discussed at a more general Meeting, and I was ordered to write you a Letter of Thanks from them for your many and judicious Observations.

When Mr. Powell communicated to me his first account of the Brecknockshire Society for Premiums which was in April last, at our next Meeting after my receiving his letter I communicated the Contents to our Society: the design was approved by all present and some of them wished that County Societies for Premiums were established throughout the Kingdom for they thought that they would exceedingly concur with the Design of a National Premium Society. On which, as a Wellwisher to the Interest of our Affairs, I sent Mr. Powell the Rules and Orders of a Philosophical Society late at Northampton of which I was formerly many years a Member, which were the Rules Mr. Powell mentioned in his Letter as being of some service. I own I have many Times since been a hearty Wellwisher to that Design but since I have received your last Letter, from the unanswerable arguments in it, I have concluded to be no ways Instrumental in promoting the Undertaking than in compliance with the orders of our Society at one of their Boards.

Any Intelligence that I can give you concerning either Mr. Powell's Plan, or any other of our Affairs which I think of Importance shall be communicated the very first Opportunity. I am with the greatest Deference to your late Sentiments on our Affairs, and also on all other Occasions I shall acquiesce in your Judgement and am with great Respect

Sir,

Your most humble,
and most obedient servant,

WILLIAM SHIPLEY[24]

Within a day or two of having written this letter to Whitworth, Shipley received one from Powell, who was delighted at the honour done to him by the Society. 'They are extremely welcome to the Copy such as it is,' wrote Powell, modestly begging that 'it may undergo a Strict Examination and be altered abridged and corrected in such Manner as may best answer the desired end'. Shipley sent a transcription to Whitworth on the 9th and received a reply written on the 15th, suggesting some amendments to Powell's proposals.[25] He read both it and Powell's letter to a meeting of the Society held on 17th September. The Society appears to have noted Whitworth's suggested amendments but not to have accepted them, for Henry Baker was given the task of preparing Powell's paper for publication, and it appeared in the November issue of the *Gentleman's Magazine* much in the form in which it had been received by Shipley three months before.[26]

Whitworth had in the meantime turned his attention to the Society's colonial correspondence and to drawing up regulations for the conduct of its meetings. Shipley received letters from him devoted to both these subjects.[27] In November he came to London for the meeting of Parliament, and was thus able to attend the Society's meetings. In the winter of 1755–6 he did much to assist Shipley in conducting the administration of the Society. Their difference of opinion over county societies did not affect what Garden called their 'close friendship'. Whitworth seems to have blocked the publication of another communication from Powell in May 1756.[28] But he was not able to persuade the Society to accept his plan for county branches. During the following thirty years county premium societies were established throughout the kingdom and Shipley, with characteristic persistence, retained his belief in their efficacy. In the 1780s, as will be seen, he was himself to be a founder of such a society in Kent, while at the same time working hard on behalf of the national society in London. Then he would be the senior and most respected member, accountable only to himself for his opinions. But in the 1750s and '60s, as Secretary and Register, he had to appear as the mouthpiece of the whole body of the subscribers and translate their decisions into action.

[ix] Secretary and Register, 1755–60

William Shipley was the principal administrative officer of the Society of Arts from 1755 to 1760. During that time the Society expanded both its membership roll and its prize-giving fund at a tremendous rate. In the first two months following the election of officers in February 1755 the number of its members rose from 17 to 81, and by 1760 a total approaching 2,000 had been reached. The Society's income increased proportionately. £360 was subscribed in 1755 and £3,482 in 1760.[1] When he gave up his duties at the end of this period, Shipley expressed his joy and pleasure at the 'great success' of the Society 'in so short a Time, increased to no middle Degree of Greatness'. With his usual modesty he claimed no credit for himself, apologising for his 'imperfect service[s] which have often been so very defective as rather to deserve your Censure than your unanimous Thanks'.[2] Modern writers have conjectured, presumably on the basis of this apology, that Shipley was a faulty administrator.[3] The records of the Socitey suggest that he provided conscientiously for its expanding needs.

At the beginning of 1755 Shipley was performing on a voluntary basis the duties which were afterwards shared amongst four officers—the Secretary, the Assistant Secretary, the Register and the Collector. Some idea of the scope of his responsibilities may be gained from the Rules and Orders which the Society adopted in 1760 and which were intended to govern the work of these officers:[4]

Business of the Secretary

He shall attend all Meetings and Committees of the Society; he shall take down all Minutes, and produce them, fairly written, at the next ensuing Meetings. He shall read all Letters and other Papers, sent or communicated to the Society, and translate them into English, if they should be in another language. He shall prepare all Answers, when ordered by the Society, in such language as shall be directed, and lay the same before the Committee appointed for their Examination . . .[5] He shall prepare all Lists of Premiums, Lists of Members, Advertisements, and other publications ordered by the Society and take care that the same be properly and correctly printed; and his Name, or that of the Assistant Secretary, as by Order of the Society, shall be signed to all Publications. He shall make proper Indexes to all the Books of the Society. He shall visit Manufactories, or apply to Manufacturers for Information, when required by the Society; and he shall, as much as possible, endeavour to make himself acquainted with the Nature and Circumstances of the several Arts and Manufactures of this and other Countries. . . .[6]

Business of the Assistant Secretary

The Assistant Secretary shall attend at all Meetings of the Society. He shall likewise attend Committees, when particularly ordered. He shall transcribe fair all the Proceedings of the Society's Meetings and Committees . . .[7] He shall transcribe all Letters that have been prepared by the Secretary, and approved by the Society. . . .[6]

Business of the Register

The Register shall have an Apartment in the House of the Society, that he may be ready on the Spot to receive Messages, Letters and all Matters brought to the Society: to answer all Inquiries, and deliver Plans, Lists, etc., to such Members as shall come or send for them, of which he shall take care to have a sufficient Number. He shall have the Custody and Care of all the Furniture, Books, such Papers as the Society shall think proper, and other Effects whatever belonging to the Society. He shall have the Direction of all the inferior Servants. He shall receive and have charge of all Matters sent to the Society by Candidates for Premiums, and shall enter them properly, at the Time when delivered, in a Book for that Purpose. He shall keep a fair Inventory of all the Goods and Effects of the Society, to be always ready when called for. He shall keep an Account of all Stationery Ware, printed Books, Coals, Candles, and all other Particulars sent by Tradesmen for the Use of the Society, in a Day-Book for that Purpose; and shall enter the same fairly, under their several Heads, in another Book, to be laid every month before the Committee of Accompts, as a Check on Trades-

men's Bills. He shall attend all Meetings and Committees of
the Society, and inform them of all Matters under his
Department, necessary for them to know. . . .[6]

Business of the Collector

The Collector shall give such security as the Society shall
require, for the Trust reposed in him. He shall collect the
Subscription Money from the Members as it becomes
due. . . .[8]

The first move towards establishing this staff of Officers
occurred at a meeting of the Society on 16th July 1755. The
minutes record that 'some Gentlemen present'[9] took notice
that Shipley could only perform his secretarial duties 'in
proper time' if he neglected his own affairs, and he was
authorised to engage clerical assistance at the expense of the
Society. Shipley seems to have been loath to take the initiative
in increasing the Society's expenses, for he was still without
assistance on 26th November, when 'the great Trouble of
Mr. Shipley in taking Minutes, writing Letters, waiting on
new Members etc. also his Expenses being observed by the
Gentlemen present, it was thought necessary to consider of
some method of giving him new Assistance'. 'The Method of
doing it' was to be settled at a General Meeting on 10th December. At that meeting an Assistant Secretary, Mr. George
Box, was appointed and it was settled that Shipley should
receive 1s. in the guinea for the subscriptions he collected,
provided this did not exceed £20 a year. A week later a committee was set up to 'consider what will be proper and reasonable to allow Mr. Shipley, the Secretary, for his trouble in
attending the several candidates whilst they are drawing for
the Premiums; and also for the use of his Room,[10] Firing,
etc.'. A fee of six guineas, 'being the sum mentioned' by

Shipley, was recommended by the Committee and confirmed by the Society on 14th January 1756. Shipley was re-elected Secretary for a further year on 3rd March. At the conclusion of his term of office he submitted a bill for £26 6s. in accordance with these arrangements.[11]

'*Present*, Mr. Shipley, Secretary and Mr. Box, Assistant Secretary.' Such an entry occurred in the Society's Minutes for the last time on 2nd March 1757. It was the general meeting appointed for 'Balloting for the several Officers of this Society for the Year ensuing', and without preamble or explanation the minutes record that Shipley was unanimously elected 'Register' of the Society and Box took the title of Secretary. Three months later the salaries of both offices were fixed at £50 a year.[12] In 1758 the secretarial salary was increased[13] but Shipley's remained unaltered down to his retirement from office at the end of 1760. The duties of the Register were those specified in the Society's 'Rules and Orders' already quoted. But in addition to the routine work of arranging meetings and caring for the Society's premises and effects, the office entailed, during Shipley's tenure, certain responsibilities of a special character.

In June 1757 the Society decided to offer a premium of £50 for a hand-worked corn mill and thus assist the poor to avoid the 'Impositions of Millers in grinding corn'.[14] So many machines were submitted that special premises were required for testing them. Shipley undertook all the arrangements and was in charge of similar experiments held in 1758.[15] In the summer of 1759 he was involved in the great upheaval of moving the Society's effects from Castle Court to Denmark Court. The new premises were more spacious than the old, but they required considerable alterations and repairs, which took several months to complete. The accommodation included a meeting room large enough to hold 400 people, a museum or 'Repository', and three other public rooms. Shipley, as

Register, seems to have put up with a minimum space, using part of the Repository as his kitchen and of the Laboratory as his pantry.[16]

The new meeting room was to become the scene of another extraordinary activity by the Society, in which Shipley must have taken a prominent part. This was the public exhibition of the works of living British artists which was held from 21st April to 3rd May 1760. One hundred and thirty works of art by sixty-nine artists were put on display. It has been estimated that over 20,000 persons visited the exhibition.[17] The crowded attendance imposed a considerable burden on the officers of the Society, who found it difficult to control the behaviour of a public unused to free art exhibitions. Windows were broken and blows exchanged. During an enquiry held into one of the incidents, Mr. Shipley gave in evidence that there were several 'irregularities committed by Persons who came to see the Exhibition'.[18] Yet Shipley was no doubt gratified at this display of public interest in the arts he was so anxious to foster. Among the exhibits was a fine portrait of him by his pupil Cosway (see illustrations).

Although Shipley had shed his Secretarial duties in March 1757, he continued to be the Society's 'Collector' as well as its Register until November 1758, and was not relieved of complete responsibility for this office until March 1760. At first his chief concern had been to enlist new members of the Society and to collect from them their initial payments.[19] The burden of this task grew with the years. Then came the added worry of obtaining subscriptions from existing members; by November 1758 arrears due to the Society amounted to £624 5s. An investigating committee recommended that Box should be paid to assist Shipley in the work of collecting subscriptions, and the Society approved this recommendation.[20] The care of monies paid to the Society was the responsibility of the Treasurer. The first holder of this honorary office was

John Goodchild, a foundation member. When Goodchild died in January 1757 Shipley took over the office for two weeks, until the son of the late Treasurer, John Goodchild II, agreed to succeed to it.[21] The second John Goodchild served as Treasurer for two years, until he was removed from the Office because of his debts. The duty of receiving money was then shared between Shipley and Box, and at their own suggestion they gave security 'for duly accounting for all such Sum and Sums of Money as they shall receive for the Use of the Society'.

Shipley's security was £100. The names of his guarantors have some intrinsic interest. They were: 'William Davies, Esq., Twyford, Hants.', and 'Charles Lawrence, Esq., Essex Street, Strand'.[22] Davies was his maternal uncle. The use of his name shows that Shipley had preserved his family links with Twyford. Lawrence, it may be recalled, attended the first meeting of the Society, and then disappeared from its proceedings. His standing security for Shipley suggests a personal association with the Founder which may well explain the mystery of his presence at Rawthmell's.[23]

Shipley shared the task of receiving subscriptions until 4th March 1760, when Box was elected to the newly created office of 'Collector', and took over complete responsibility for this work. The change had been recommended by a Committee 'to consider what Officers are necessary and Proper for the Society', which had been set up two months before. Another of its recommendations led to the election of a new Secretary in Box's place. Box was given the title of 'Assistant Secretary' as well as that of 'Collector'. As for Shipley, the Committee reported that 'the present Register is a very proper Person to be continued in that Office'.[24]

Trueman Wood conjectured that Shipley may not have liked the 'new conditions' and that this dissatisfaction may have been a cause of his resignation six months later.[25] There is no evidence to support this conjecture. The office of Register remained the same in duties and remuneration as it had been before the new appointments. Only its precedence in the printed 'Lists of the Society' was altered. Instead of the Officers being listed as 'Mr. William Shipley, *Register*, Mr. George Box, *Secretary*', they now appeared in the following order:

> Templeman, Dr. Peter, *Secretary*,
> Box, Mr. George, *Assistant Secretary*,
> Shipley, Mr. William, *Register*,
> Box, Mr. George, *Collector*.[26]

If this apparent diminution in the prestige of his office gave Shipley any grounds for discontent, he would surely have consoled himself with the knowledge that the Society had conferred on him two honours which distinguished him from

The Gold Medal awarded to Shipley by the Society in 1758 (from the engraving on the title-page of Thomas Mortimer's Concise Account)

its other Officers. In 1755, it may be recalled, he had been elected a 'Perpetual Member' of the Society. The Society's 'Rules and Orders' of 1760 laid down that 'neither the Secretary, Assistant Secretary, the Register, nor the Collector of Subscriptions, shall be members of the Society', but they specifically exempted 'Mr. Shipley, the present Register'.[27] In 1758 the Society began to bestow medals as honorary rewards. Henry Baker had sponsored the idea in 1756 and it had also been advocated in Shipley's 'Scheme'. Some time elapsed before a satisfactory design could be composed and a die cast, but by 24th May 1758 all was ready, and gold medals were duly presented to Lords Folkestone and Romney on that day.

During the course of the year three silver medals were awarded for drawing and afforestation and two more gold medallists were nominated. The more valuable awards went to the Duke of Beaufort for planting acorns and to James Stuart, 'Painter and Architect . . . for designing this medal'.[28] Then on 13th December 'A Motion was made . . . That a Gold Medal be presented to Mr. Shipley, which was unanimously agreed to [and the Society] Ordered, that it be referred to the Committee of Premiums to consider of proper Inscriptions'. A week later the minutes record that 'Mr. Israel Wilkes reported from the Committee of Premiums that they are of opinion, that the following Inscriptions be engraved on the Gold Medal, which is to be presented to Mr. Shipley. Viz. without the Wreath of Olive TO WILLIAM SHIPLEY. Within the Wreath WHOSE PUBLIC SPIRIT AND PERSEVERANCE GAVE RISE TO THIS SOCIETY'. The Committee's suggestions were adopted, except for the words underlined, and Shipley was presented with this tangible token of his greatest achievement.

The goodwill of the Society towards Shipley was shown again on the occasion of his resignation from the office of Register on 1st October 1760. After his letter of resignation had been read,[29] it was 'ordered unanimously that the Thanks of the Society be given to Mr. Shipley for his Diligence and Fidelity in the Execution of his Office; and thanks were accordingly returned to him from the Chair'. There were to be many occasions in the future when the Society of Arts would express thanks to its founder.

75

[x] 'Shipley's School', 1753–8

It has been seen that Shipley's dual rôle as the senior founding member and chief administrative officer of the Society occasionally caused him some anxiety. Apparently more difficult to reconcile must have been his position as the promoter of a disinterested public society for the encouragement of the arts with his proprietorship of a private drawing school whose pupils were often successful in obtaining the monetary prizes voted out of the funds subscribed by the Society. The case against him in its blackest form would have suggested that his object in founding the Society of Arts was simply to advance his fortunes as an art teacher. Historians have taken care to rebut this charge and the circumstances of his life as already related have shown its falsity. Nevertheless it is surprising that more was not made of it at the time. Grub Street liked to expose projectors and their projects. But in its early years the Society of Arts received a very good press. That there was much public good will towards the new Society was shown by the rapid rise in the numbers of its subscribers in its early years. The fact that it had as its Secretary and Register a man who was tireless in his work on its behalf and who was content with a modest and unasked-for salary no doubt helped its reputation. Nor were its activities confined to the arts of drawing and painting. Mechanical, agricultural and commercial arts were also encouraged. This had been Shipley's plan, and he was active in promoting many of the scientific and economic aspects of the Society's work. Yet it cannot be denied that, during the period of Shipley's active association with the Society, rewarding the 'polite arts' grew to be one of its principal activities, that a number of celebrated artists took part in its proceedings and even laid before it a scheme for establishing a national academy of arts, and that in 1760 it sponsored the first public exhibition of the works of British painters. The uninitiated could be pardoned for assuming that the Society of Arts was also a Society of Artists[1] and that success in that profession could be assured by attending the school kept by the man who was identified with the Society. Perhaps it was only in the scrupulously honest mind of Shipley that a clear distinction could be drawn between them. In the early months when the Society and the Drawing School were both in their infancy the distinction was unimportant.

Shipley continued to lodge at his friend Husband Messiter's until March 1755, when he took a house in Craig's Court.[2] He cannot have had much time to practise his profession as a painter or a drawing master while he was occupied with the foundation of the Society. Yet he did solicit business, as can be seen from the advertisement he inserted in the *Northampton Mercury* on 27th May 1754:

> WILLIAM SHIPLEY, Painter,
> Lately resident at Northampton,
> BEING obliged to settle in London, takes this opportunity to thank the Nobility, Gentry, and Others, who have favoured him with their Commands; and to acquaint them, that any Orders, directed to him, at Mr. Messiter's, Surgeon, in Great Pulteney Street, near Golden Square, will be punctually executed.[3]

This advertisement followed immediately after one announcing the formation of the Society of Arts and offering the premiums for producing cobalt and madder and for 'the best Drawings, by Boys and Girls, under the age of 14 years, and Proof of their abilities, on or before the 15th day of January, 1755 . . . Likewise for the best Drawings by Boys and Girls, between the ages of 14 and 17'.

The five successful claimants for the awards offered for drawings from the younger age group—Richard Cosway, John

Smart, J. A. Gresse, Barbara Marsden and J. A. Porter—were, according to Dossie, 'instructed by and under the direction of Mr. William Shipley'.[4] This means that Shipley had begun to take pupils while he was lodging at Messiter's. Early in December 1754 he had arranged for young Richard Cosway to come up to London from Tiverton.[5] The boy became his most successful pupil and seems to have lived with him in his various homes during the next five years.[6] The dates when the other four successful competitors began their studies under Shipley cannot be determined. All that can be said with certainty is that by 15th January 1755 he had at least five pupils. Dossie states that 'the majority' of the five successful competitors for the 14 to 17 age group were instructed by another drawing master, so that it is not possible to add to Shipley's total from this source.[7]

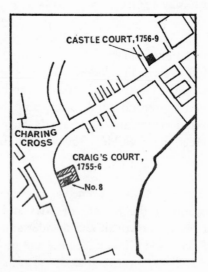

Sketch map of Charing Cross and the western part of the Strand showing premises shared by Shipley's School and the Society of Arts, 1755–9. Beaufort Buildings were on the southern side of the Strand, just beyond the top right-hand corner of the map

78

There were, however, twenty-eight boys and seven girls who were unsuccessful in the competition and some of them may also have studied under Shipley. All candidates had access to his 'Collection of Prints, Pictures, Drawings, Models, etc.'.[8]

At No. 8 Craig's Court, which Shipley sub-let to the Society from March 1755 until June 1756, he had the use of the Society's rooms 'when the Society does not meet there'. His Drawing School now shared with his Society their first regular establishment. When the candidates attended to compete for the 1756 drawing awards Shipley provided a room for them to work in and acted as an invigilator.[9] Fourteen candidates were given prizes. Amongst them were five of Shipley's pupils, Gresse, Marsden and Smart of the 1755 group and two new names, William Pars and Simon Taylor.[10] In August 1756 Shipley showed his satisfaction at his pupils' progress in a letter to Dr. Garden which called forth a reply from South Carolina requesting as 'a most singular favour to have some copies of your young pupils, which I would endeavour to make good use of'.[11] The fame of Shipley's school was beginning to spread.

The next house to be shared by the School and the Society was one of the largest in the Strand. It was situated at the corner of Castle Court, and was the property of a general domestic and estate agency, known as the 'Universal Register Office', which had been started as a scheme of public utility by John Fielding, the blind magistrate, and his half-brother, Henry Fielding, the novelist (d. 1754). For the rent of £36 15s. paid by the Society, the Universal Register Office made over to it what was described as 'One large Room on the first floor . . . abutting on the Strand, One small Room adjoining to the said Large room and the one other Room on the same floor. . . . One Garret, one Kitchen on the Ground Floor and one Cellar Under Ground'.[12]

The large room was used for Society meetings, and the

small ones for Committees, and by Shipley for his School and for residential purposes. Shipley was allowed free use of this accommodation by the Society as a partial recompense for his extensive labours as its chief administrator, and this arrangement was given formal sanction in March 1757, when he was appointed Register of the Society, and entitled *ex officio* to 'an apartment in the House of the Society'.[13]

The work of his school at this time was described in a notice published in the *Public Advertiser* in June 1757:[14]

> Drawing in all its branches taught by William Shipley, Register of the Society for the Encouragement of Arts, Manufacturers and Commerce, and other proper Masters at the above Society's Office.
>
> As it will be Mr. Shipley's endeavour to introduce Boys and Girls of Genius to Masters and Mistresses in such Manufactures as require Fancy and Ornament, and for which the Knowledge of Drawing is absolutely necessary; Masters or Mistresses who want Boys or Girls well qualified for such manufactures may frequently meet with them at this School; and Parents who have Children of good natural Abilities for the Art of Drawing may here meet with Opportunities of having them well instructed and recommended to proper Masters or Mistresses, by applying to Mr. Shipley, at Mr. Bailey's,[15] the corner of Castle Street, opposite to the New Exchange Buildings in the Strand.
>
> A genteel Apartment is provided for the reception of Young Ladies of Fashion, who are attended every day from Eleven to one.

Shipley expressed in his notice the same concern with the use of drawing in industry as was intended by the Society's Premiums 'for the most ingenious and best fancied Designs proper for Weavers, Embroiderers and Calico Printers'. In

1756 and 1757 his pupils competed successfully for these premiums and although many of them later became professional artists,[10] their parents had no doubt been reassured by the statement composed by Shipley and Baker for the *Gentleman's Magazine* that 'the Society would not be misunderstood to aim at raising numbers of what are usually called Painters'.[16]

Young Ozias Humphry of Honiton had a passion for drawing and almost 'wearied his parents by his importuning' that he might be sent away to a Drawing School. Their resistance was overcome by the appearance of one of Shipley's advertisements in a Barnstaple newspaper, and at the age of fifteen Ozias was sent up to London on the understanding that he would learn to draw patterns suitable for the family lace business.[17] On the 6th September 1757 he wrote home to his father and mother: 'I have been to Mr. Shipley's School all last week and I like it very well and have entered myself this Day accordingly.'[18]

From the boy's correspondence with his mother information can be derived about the fees and curriculum at Shipley's School. 'Half a Guinea Entrance and a Guinea a month for two Days in a week' was what young Ozias had to pay, and his mother thought it 'a great deal of money'.[19] Paper and pencils were supplied as extras although Ozias asked to be allowed to use his own: 'Mr. Shipley' told him 'that there is never a Scholar that does but if you chuse it you may'. Ozias described 'the Particulars of Mr. Shipley's drawing School' as 'Men's Heads, and Plaster Figures, Birds on Trees, Landscapes, all sorts of Beasts, Flowers, foliages and Ornaments'.[20] He explained to his mother that 'the reason of my being so eager to enter myself at Mr. Shipley's School was because I knew that drawing of Heads etc. must give me a truer idea in Drawing Lace Patterns'.[21] By the end of October he was being allowed to copy lace patterns and was well pleased with his general progress. 'Our Usher,' he wrote, 'affirms that there is no scholar in our School has made so great a Progress in learning to draw as I have.'[22]

Mrs. Humphry seems to have concluded that her son had, within a period of a few months at Shipley's school, learnt all that was necessary, and on 15th February 1758 she wrote to him settling his return to Honiton and warning him 'to pay Mr. Shipley only about 2 or 3 days before your quarter is out; then do you have a bill and receipt in full and be sure to behave yourself Genteel to every Person that you have been acquainted with.'[23] Evidently she thought that Shipley might neglect his pupil if he knew that he was to be withdrawn from his school. Nothing could have been farther from Shipley's character. When Ozias wrote to him later in the year enquiring about the possibility of resuming his studies in London, the boy received the following reply, as meticulous in courtesy and informative detail as a letter intended for some distinguished correspondent of the Society of Arts:

Sir,

I received your letter and had answered it sooner but have been closely engaged in attending the Candidates for our Handmills who have lately produced their various contrivances for the Premium of £50 offered this year by our Society for the Cheapest and best Handmill.

In answer to your query concerning our Drawing Premiums I think the most proper Classes for you to draw in are viz.

For a Human Figure or for the best Drawings of Birds, Beasts, Fruit, Flowers etc. In the former class the Candidates Drawings must be copied from a Print or Drawing and the subject an Academy Figure by Boys under the Age of eighteen, in the latter class the drawings are to be taken from Nature by Boys under the age of seventeen.

Should your Father think proper for you to come again

to London to improve yourself further in the Art of Drawing, I assure you that now you may have greater opportunities, at present, of perfecting your studies than when you was last in London. For the Duke of Richmond has opened an Academy which is filled with casts of the most capital of the Antique Statues from which any Boy being properly recommended may draw gratis.[24]

Our school flourishes very much at present and I have at very great expense procured a great number of capital Drawings and my new Assistant Mr. Burgess is perhaps as good a Draughtsman as any in the Kingdom.

Your old friend W. Pars sends his humble service to you and says that you shall shortly hear from him by a young Gentleman who is going to Exeter, and I am with compliments to your Papa and Mama,

Sir, Your very humble servant,

W. SHIPLEY

P.S. In making your Premium Drawing you are allowed to have the best Instructions you can get, but it is to be entirely your own performance without being touched by anybody whatsoever, and is to be sent directed to me before the second Wednesday in January next.[25]

The entry conditions for the Society's fine art premiums which Shipley mentioned in the postscript to his letter had been settled soon after the judging of the 1758 competition. They provided for radical change in Shipley's relations to the candidates. Hitherto it had been laid down that 'all candidates for pecuniary premiums are required to draw at the Society's Office under the inspection of a person to be appointed by the Society [i.e. William Shipley]'. But although Shipley had a good collection of casts and prints which the Society authorised him to enlarge, his collection could not, of course, stand comparison with the Duke of Richmond's. Furthermore, he

did not employ living models, who were generally considered too difficult for the younger students to copy. So that
when the Society decided that for its 1759 competition it would
admit candidates who drew from the life in the St. Martin's
Lane Academy or copied any statue in the Duke of Richmond's
gallery, and that all others 'may draw or model at their respective dwellings', his direct connection with the competitions
came to an end.[26] It will be seen, however, that in the years
1759–61 his pupils won a number of important awards, and
that his School continued to prosper.

[xi] Shipley's School, 1758–68

In spite of the intention of Shipley, through his School, and
of the Society of Arts, through its premiums, to train boys and
girls in drawing for trades and manufactures, they both
assisted in the nurture of professional artists. Ozias Humphry,
though not a premium winner, is an example of one of Shipley's pupils who turned away from his intended career as a
lace-pattern designer to become a successful miniature and
portrait painter. Of the six of Shipley's pupils who won
premiums for designing textiles, one became a portrait painter,
one a botanical illustrator, one an architect, one gave up her
career for marriage and another became a glass ornament
cutter. The latter is the only one of Shipley's twenty-one
identified pupils who can be said to have worked at a trade.
A list in the appendix analyses their occupations. Some reserve
is needed in its interpretation. For it is naturally easier to
identify the pupils who made a name in the fine arts than those
who followed more anonymous professions. However, the
list does testify to the value of Shipley's instruction for a wide
range of accomplishment in the fine arts, including sculpture
and architecture.

J. T. Smith[1] related that his father, Nathaniel Smith, and

Joseph Nollekens, the sculptors, 'were playfellows and both learned drawing together at Shipley's school, then kept in the Strand at . . . the corner of Castle Court'. There they met Cosway, the miniaturist, who used to 'carry in the tea and coffee, which Mr. Shipley's housekeeper was allowed to provide and for which she charged threepence per head'. James Gandon, the architect, recalled in his autobiographical memoranda how he attended Shipley's school in the evenings when he was working as a student assistant in the office of William Chambers. Under Shipley, he 'had every opportunity of acquiring . . . a theoretic knowledge of architecture'. Shipley's School, he wrote, 'was at that period [c. 1757–60] the first in London in general estimation. Many of the most eminent painters and architects received their first instructions there'. But Gandon also had as his fellow students 'many [who] embarked in other professions, amongst others my friend Henderson [the actor] and my valued and esteemed friend, Captain Grosse, the eminent antiquarian'.[2]

At the end of June 1759 the Society of Arts removed its effects from the house at the corner of Castle Court to a newly built headquarters in Denmark Court, farther eastward in the Strand. Shipley, as Register, was given residential accommodation in the new building, and lived there at least until December 1760, when he retired from office in the Society. It is not certain whether he also moved his Drawing School to Denmark Court.[3] If he did it would have only been for a short while, for by 1760 he had taken over another property as a school on the opposite side of the Strand. This was the magnificent 'Great Room', measuring 65 by 30 by 24 ft., a relic of Old Beaufort House, which had passed into the ownership of a Mr. Clarke.[4]

For three weeks in 1757 and for eight weeks in 1758, the Society of Arts had hired Mr. Clarke's Great Room to house the numerous hand mills which were submitted in response to the premiums it offered for improvements in these machines. Shipley had been responsible for all the arrangements and had thus become acquainted with the premises and their owner. Clarke had charged the Society a rent of one guinea a week,[5] and presumably his charge to Shipley would have been based on this estimate of the value of his Great Room. Although the rent Shipley paid is not known, it was probably at least as much as the thirty-five guineas a year the Society had paid for the premises in Castle Court. It is an indication of the profitability of his Drawing School that Shipley could afford such a rent out of his own resources and, at the end of 1760, forgo his salary from the Society.

In his letter of resignation from the office of Register, Shipley referred to his 'having lately engaged in business of such importance as to render him incapable of discharging his duty to the Society as their Register without very much injuring his own affairs'.[6] This important business was presumably the expansion of his Drawing School. Soon after he gave up his office he purchased from the Society a stock of furniture which was no doubt designed to furnish his new Great Room.[7]

Shipley's Drawing School was said to have been 'established . . . upon a more enlarged plan than had before been attempted in the Country'.[8] It seems to have enjoyed a spectacular success and to have been held in affectionate veneration by the students who attended it. Yet just as Shipley gave up his post as Register when the success of the Society was assured, so he soon retired from the active management of the School. Thomas Jones, the Welsh landscape painter, wrote that he 'went to London in November, 1761, to commence upon my novitiate at Mr. Shipley's School . . . which he [Shipley] had a little time before consigned over to Mr. Henry Pars assisted occasionally by his brother William Pars'.[9] Thus the date of Shipley's retirement from the School must have been within a year of his retirement from the Society.

William Pars was only nineteen in 1761. He had been one of Shipley's most successful pupils and a regular premium winner of the Society since 1756. His brother Henry, eight years his senior, had been trained to follow their father's profession as a chaser. But, according to Edward Edwards, 'as chasing declined in fashion',[10] Henry Pars took up the teaching of drawing and painting. He was to be the principal of Shipley's School for at least thirty years and to maintain the reputation which its founder had given it.[11] The following newspaper advertisement was published by the Pars brothers in 1762:

Drawing and Modelling in all branches taught by Henry and William Pars, successors to Mr. Shipley, late Register to the Society for the Encouragement of Arts etc., and other proper masters, at Mr. Clarke's Great Room, near Beaufort Buildings in the Strand, where Boys of genius are frequently recommended to masters in such trades and manufactures as require fancy and ornament, for which the knowledge of drawing is absolutely necessary . . . Mr. Shipley will still be willing to recommend young people educated at this school according to their genius and improvement.[12]

The last sentence shows that Shipley continued to take an interest in his former School after he had retired from active management. It would be characteristic of him to wish to continue encouraging youthful talent. Thomas Jones, whom Shipley had taught by correspondence, described his experiences in London in 1761 and 1762 as a student at what had then become Pars's school.

Here I was reduced to the humiliating situation of copying drawings of Ears, Eyes, Mouths and Noses among a group of little boys of half my age who had had the start of me by two or three years. This spurred me to greater Exertion—

and in a few months, being thought sufficiently qualified, I was introduced by Mr. Shipley to the Duke of Richmond's Gallery in Privy Gardens, to draw after those fine copies of the most celebrated Antique Statues. . . . In October, 1762, I was admitted a member of the Academy for Drawing after living models . . . in . . . St. Martin's Lane.[13]

William Burgess, a former member of the staff of Shipley's School, had by 1762 established a school of his own and taken with him some of Pars's pupils. When these students entered for the Society's competition in April 1762, Burgess wrote to the Society saying he 'hoped that they may not be intimidated by Mr. Shipley who is offended at their being taken from his late school in the Strand'.[14] Clearly Shipley still had the interests of his School at heart in 1762. In *The Universal Director* for 1763 he appears as a 'Landscape Painter' of whom enquiries could be made at Pars's School. By 1765 he was being listed by the Society of Arts as 'Mr. William Shipley, Gent.', residing in Lyon's Inn, which means he was again living on the north side of the Strand.[15] There he remained till his final move away from London in 1768, and in the meantime he had been busy at the Society in his new rôle as an independent member.

[*xii*] *Relations with the Society of Arts, 1760–78*

As long as he held the office of Register, Shipley was not usually listed as being present at meetings of the Society's Committees. But after his resignation from that office on 1st October 1760 he exercised his right as a member to attend such Committees as interested him,[1] and the Committee Minute Books for the next eight years record his presence at 151 meetings. He attended 16 times in the Society's session for 1760–1, 26 times in 1761–2 and 34 times in 1762–3, and 36 times in 1763–4. For the session 1764–5 his attendances dropped to 10 but rose again to 23 for 1765–6. In 1766–7 and 1767–8, the two sessions preceding his move to Maidstone, he attended three times in each. Unlike the majority of members, Shipley took part in the work of all the nine standing Committees of the Society during this period, although some Committees clearly interested him more than others. As would be expected, his attendances were greatest at the Committee of Polite Arts, amounting to a total of 68 for the whole period, 1760–8; next came the Committee of Mechanics with 28 attendances, then the Committee of Chemistry with 16 and the Committee of Manufactures with 10. He attended 9 times each at the Committees of Agriculture and Miscellaneous matters. His lowest attendance totals were reserved for the Committee of Colonies and Trade (3) and the two administrative Committees, Correspondence (5) and Accounts (2). Perhaps Shipley felt that he had had more than his fair share of the latter aspects of the Society's work when he had been Secretary and Register? Colonial development certainly interested him, as was proved by his correspondence with Dr. Garden, but he would hardly have regarded himself as an authority on the subject, whereas his standing as an artist and inventor qualified him to serve on the other 'Premium Committees'. The minutes did not record individual Committee members' contributions to debate. If Joseph Moser is to be believed, Shipley would have been generally 'reserved, distant and, indeed, silent to extreme', though he could be drawn by a congenial companion to talk at length on 'the rise and progress of, and the improvement that had been, and might be, made in a variety of arts and manufactures'.[2] Yet if all Shipley did was to countenance the Committee meetings by his presence, his formidable attendance record would be sufficient to show that he had honoured his promise 'to use his utmost endeavours to promote the Interest of this Society as a member thereof'.[3]

As well as attending the Society's Committees, Shipley was

no doubt also present at its ordinary and general meetings. The minutes of these meetings ceased to record the names of attending members after 1757, so it is impossible to determine how often Shipley was present at them after his resignation as Register. In 1762 and 1763, however, his name figures in the Minutes as the author of two suggestions for action by the Society which show that he was far from being a passive witness of its proceedings.

On 12th May 1762 he laid before the Society a plan for setting up a 'Repository' or gallery, financed by the Society, where artists 'may copy such original pictures and other works of Art as may be deposited for that purpose'. The Committee of Polite Arts, to whom the plan was referred by the Society, met to give it consideration on the 15th May and declared it to be 'an object worthy the attention of the Society'. They recommended 'that Convenient Rooms or Apartments near the Society's Office be hired proper for a secure Repository, and for the Artists to paint or draw in'. The Committee's report was read at a meeting of the Society on the 19th and recommitted with a request for details of the 'Extent of the Design and the Expence'. Shipley worked these out with great care and submitted them to a meeting of the Committee on the 21st. The minutes record that:

> Mr. Shipley acquainted the Committee that the Tenant of Essex House had agreed to let three Rooms on the second Floor for £20 Per Annum . . .
>
> That there be ten Chairs in the Great Room of the said House at 2s and 6d Each.
>
> That £5 be allowed for the furnishing the Committee Room,
>
> That £3 be allowed for the Chairwoman,
>
> That £3. 3. 0. be allowed for Packing Cases,
>
> That £5. 5. 0. be allowed for Porterage,

That £12. 7. o. be allowed for Coals and Contingencies,

That £50 Per Annum be allowed to the Superintendent.
. . . It is the opinion of this Committee that Mr. Shipley's Design may be carried into Execution for the Annual Expense of £100 including a proper Superintendent and all other necessary Disbursements.[4]

The Committee expressed their belief that Shipley's proposed Repository 'would especially contribute to the advancement of the Arts of Painting and Drawing in various branches of the Polite Arts and in its consequences improve in many articles the ornamental Manufactures of these Kingdoms'. Unfortunately their recommendations failed to pass the scrutiny of a Society meeting held on 14th June. The reason for rejection is not recorded in the minutes, but may have derived from the anxiety caused at that date by the near collapse of the Meeting Room.[5] At a time when extra money was needed for repairs and for hiring a temporary meeting room, the Society would have been unlikely to welcome the commitments involved in establishing and running a repository of Arts. The unlucky circumstances prevented it from taking what would have been a significant step in the history of English art education. Had the Society adopted Shipley's proposal, it might well have established an institution which would have replaced the Duke of Richmond's gallery, then 'on the decline',[6] foreshadowed the Royal Academy as a centre for art teaching, and provided a wonderful nucleus for a national gallery of British painting.

Shipley's second suggestion arose out of some research he appears to have undertaken into the migration of fish around the coasts of Kent and Essex in 1762. The public promotion of the British fisheries was a favourite topic amongst seventeenth- and eighteenth-century economic writers. The Crown and Parliament had made various attempts to encourage the fisheries, and in 1750 the 'Society of the Free British Fishery' had been established.[7] The Secretary of this company was John Lockman, the 'Herring Poet',[8] who became an active member of the Society of Arts.

The Society itself had offered premiums for sturgeon (1760), turbots (1762) and cured stockfish (1762).[9] Shipley wanted it 'to attempt the increase of fish in general on the sea coast, by stocking each part with such kinds as are not now found there'.[10] A special Committee of the Society (including amongst its members John Lockman) met to consider his proposal on 1st February 1763.[11] The practicability of the scheme 'was disputed by some and maintained by others',[12] but the majority of the Committee Members felt that it would be prudent to concentrate on one species only, and a resolution was passed suggesting that the Society should accept Shipley's plan for encouraging the establishment of 'Pits or Beds for Scallops as near as they properly can be to London, so as to supply the markets thereof'.[13] For, as Dossie later explained, scallops 'being a heavy shell fish, could not remove again easily from the places where they were required to stay and breed'.[12] The Society accepted the Committee's recommendation and premiums for scallops were offered accordingly.

Between April 1768 and November 1778 Shipley appears to have been present at only one meeting of a Committee of the Society. He was evidently in London on 28th April 1772, as his name is listed among those present at the Committee of Mechanics on that day. But apart from this isolated occasion he was no doubt generally prevented from visiting the capital by his newly found domestic responsibilities at Maidstone. However, the Society had not forgotten him. During this decade, it built and moved into the present headquarters in the Adelphi, and in decorating the interior it determined to commemorate the founder. In 1778 the painter James Barry was authorised to include in his great scheme of paintings for the walls of the new meeting room 'the portrait of Mr. Shipley as the Founder of the Society'.[14] A year earlier, Shipley received recognition from the Society in his own right as an inventor through the receipt of one of its honorary awards.

The Society's manuscript Transactions for the Session 1776–7 record that 'A Letter of Thanks and the Silver Medal were voted to Mr. William Shipley for his ingenious and humane contrivances for saving the Lives of persons who fell overboard at sea and for presenting a Machine for that purpose to the Society'.[15] The machine was a boat-shaped air-tight float, 2 ft. 3 in. by 1 ft. 1 in. by 1 ft., made of tin plates and filled with bladders so that it would keep its buoyancy should its sides be pierced. It carried a lantern, swung to maintain a perpendicular position, and protected by a double top from the sea spray. Handles were fixed to the side of the float, and a rope ladder, to which another lantern and a special hook were attached, was supplied for use during rescue operations. More than twenty years before Shipley had designed a 'Float ... to preserve the lives of them that fall overboard at Sea' and had displayed it at a Meeting of the Society held in November 1754. The Society had 'ordered that enquiries be made of Persons skilled in Sea-Affairs', but the minutes record no further action in the matter.[16] Presumably Shipley worked on his contrivance during the subsequent period and decided to resubmit it to the Society at some appropriate moment. On 24th April 1776 he came to a meeting of the Society and delivered his float and an account of how it should be used.

An Account of the Use of a FLOATING LIGHT, *calculated to save the lives of such persons as have the misfortune to fall overboard in the night.*

It is proposed, in order to make this float useful, that it be every night under the care of those officers who are on the watch, and that its lamp be frequently trimmed and supplied with fresh oil, and its snuff moistened with oil of turpentine, that it may take fire with the least touch of a lamp or candle; and whenever the ship is alarmed by any of the sailors falling overboard in the night, the officer on watch may light the lamp in the lantern belonging to the float as

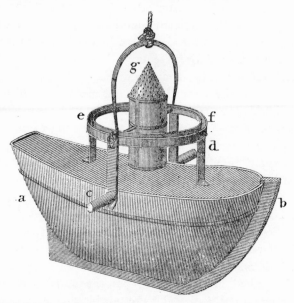

'Mr. Wm. Shipley's Floating Light.' Drawn from the inventor's model for the Society's Transactions, *Vol. XXV, plate 7*

expeditiously as possible, and let the float down by the small cord into the water, till it has floated about one second of time, and the float is a little way out of the perpendicular of the small cord; he is then to fasten the cord to the reel for the line, and toss it over-board, which will sink down and pull the line almost perpendicular, and thus it will not be liable to entangle the person when he swims to the float, who, when he has got hold of the handles of it, may move very fast which way he will, only by striking his legs in the same manner as he does when he swims; and as the light of the lamp will be a certain direction for the person overboard to find the float, so it will also direct them in the ship to find the man and float.

And when the ship has tacked about, and is come to the float, then the following method is proposed to take up the man and float into the ship, viz. the lantern with the rope-ladder may be let down from the end of a pole with a cord and pulley, till the cross-bar below the lantern touches the water, which may be seen by them in the ship by means of the light from the bottom of the lantern, and thus the man in the water may lay hold of the cross-bar, and fix his feet on one of the steps of the rope-ladder; and he may then lay hold of the iron bale of the float with one hand, and hang it on the hook of the rope above the cross-bar; which being done, by the help of a pulley fastened to the end of a pole, the man and float may be both safely lifted into the ship.[17]

The Society referred the float to the Committee of Mechanics, which duly adjudged it worthy of a silver medal. The award was confirmed at a meeting of the Society,[18] and Shipley responded with a letter of appreciation:

Maidstone Jan. 7th 1777

Gentlemen,

I have received the Silver Medal which you were pleased to order for me contriving a floating light, calculated to save the lives of them who fall overboard in the night at sea which I suppose may serve as a hint, for some mechanic Artist who is well versed in sea affairs to improve from by making a floating light so perfect, as to answer all his wished-for purposes.

This medal from you is by me more esteemed, than a very

considerable pecuniary reward would be from any other body of gentlemen; and I believe that nothing can give me more pleasure than this honorary mark of your approbation has done, unless it is to hear that my floating light is shortly used at sea and is a means of saving the lives of several of that class of people, whom all maritime powers esteem very valuable members of society, and that it may then be ranked amongst the many useful Contrivances, that have been introduced to the public under your patronage.

    I am with the greatest regard,

        Gentlemen,

                Your very humble servant,

                    WILLIAM SHIPLEY

    This letter and the description of the floating light were published by the Society in 1785 as the work of 'Mr. William Shipley, of Maidstone, whose benevolence is universally known and acknowledged'.[17] For Shipley's move from London by no means brought to an end his strivings for the public good. His life and work at Maidstone will be considered in the next chapter.

5

DISENGAGEMENT AND REINVOLVEMENT

'*For it is presumed many of the worthy inhabitants of
Kent . . . will endeavour to imitate the ingenuity and
public spirit of their forefathers, and think it inglorious
to be themselves inactive. . . .*'

Shipley's Plan to extend the Maidstone Society, 1786

[*xiii*] *Marriage and Maidstone, 1767–86*

It has been more than once asserted that Shipley was married
at Maidstone, following his retirement there in 1768.[1] The
unacknowledged authority for this belief was the oral evidence
of the grandson of one of Shipley's servants, which was taken
in the early years of the present century by J. H. Allchin,
Curator of Maidstone Museum from 1902 to 1923. From another of Allchin's informants came the story of Shipley's
arriving late for his marriage because he absentmindedly
chased after a rare butterfly on his way to the church in Maidstone.[2] Though this tradition may be of value as evidence of
popular belief in Shipley's eccentricity, it is contradicted by
the precise information regarding the place and date of
Shipley's marriage which is now available. The St. George's,
Hanover Square, Marriage Register records that he married at
that church 'Elizabeth Miller, of this Parish, Spinster', on
23rd November 1767.[3]

Who was Elizabeth Miller, and how did Shipley come to meet her? The entry in the St. George's register provides a tentative answer to these questions. A William Miller witnessed the ceremony and he was presumably the father of the bride, and therefore, like her, 'of this parish'. In the previous year, Shipley had proposed 'William Miller, Esq., Queen's Row, Pimlico' for election as a member of the Society of Arts.[4] Queen's Row was in the Parish of St. George's, and it is therefore not improbable that this was the William Miller who became Shipley's father-in-law. His interest in the Society was either the cause or the consequence of a friendship with Shipley, and this friendship most probably led to a meeting between Shipley and his daughter. The couple were both of a late age for marriage, Shipley being fifty-two and Elizabeth Miller thirty-seven. There are no letters, diaries or memoirs extant to tell of their feelings for each other, or of the special circumstances of their meeting. As will be seen, it was to be a fruitful and a lasting union, but speculation about its prompting must rest on matter-of-fact calculations of pounds, shillings and pence.

At the age of twenty-one Shipley had received the £500 legacy which had been held in trust for him since the death of his maternal grandfather, William Davies. He may have received some small legacy from his mother who died in 1757, though she had herself only inherited £300 from William Davies.[5] But until that year at least, his capital would have been unaugmented by legacies and can have grown little from his salary at the Society of Arts. It is reasonable to suppose that Shipley followed the convention of his time and only contemplated matrimony when he was certain of the means to support an enlarged household. Since he gave up all lucrative employment before his marriage and yet lived comfortably for the rest of his life, being able to bequeath £8,000 at his death,[6] it must be assumed that he increased his fortune by a considerable amount between 1757 and 1767. One source of this

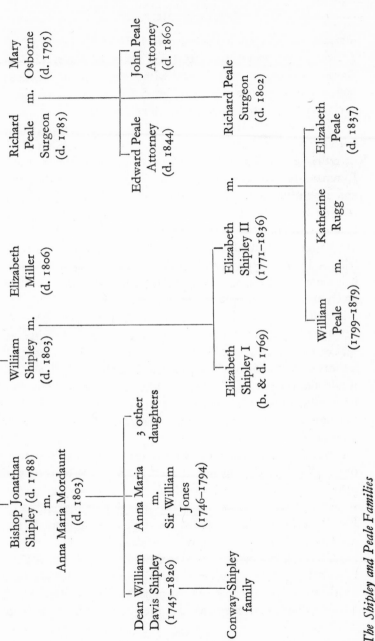

The Shipley and Peale Families

increase can be accurately determined. This was the legacy of £1,000 which he received from his maternal uncle, William Davies, Junior, in 1765.[7] Otherwise it must be assumed to have come from the profits of his School, and no accounts survive which enable these to be calculated.

Just as Shipley's marriage may be linked to an association with the Society of Arts, so his choice of Maidstone as a place of retirement probably stemmed from the same source. Lord Romney,[8] his old collaborator in the foundation of the Society, and its President since 1761, had his seat at the Mote, just outside the town. This benevolent peer may well have encouraged Shipley to settle near his estate. Their subsequent work together in the locality points to the continuance of their friendship. But whatever his reason for choosing Maidstone, it is certain that Shipley found there scope for all his interests and was content to pass the remainder of his long life in that 'pleasant, large and populous' County Town of Kent.[9]

Within a year of his marriage, Shipley was established at Maidstone. The rate books show that on 18th November 1768 he was assessed for holding property in Gabriel's Hill, a good residential quarter of the town.[10] On 3rd February 1769 his first child, Elizabeth, was baptised at All Saints' Church, but through some unhappy illness or accident died after two months. A second Elizabeth was baptised on 19th July 1771;[11] she was destined to outlive her parents and to be their only other offspring. During her father's lifetime, she married the second son and namesake of Richard Peale, the Maidstone surgeon who had been a successful champion of inoculation.[12] Richard Peale, Senior, is shown as Shipley's neighbour in the 1768 rate assessment, and the friendship between the two families probably dates from this time. Richard Peale, Junior, followed his father's profession of medicine, and his two brothers, John and Edward, became successful attorneys.[13] Shipley nominated them as the executors of his will, and although they are known to have practised law in the City of London they are also said to have been 'intimate' with Shipley[14] and to have lived with him at Knightrider House, Knightrider Street. Shipley probably came to live in this interesting residence, to which local tradition and a commemorative plaque link his name,[15] at the close of his years at Maidstone. The house belonged to the Peale family, yet Shipley paid rates as a Maidstone householder right down to his death in 1803 and rent to a local landowner until at least 1800,[16] evidence which suggests that he lived near Knightrider House but did not share it with the Peales until old age made it convenient for him and his wife to give up their own establishment.

Knightrider House stands to this day, a three-storied rectangular country town mansion, externally much as it would have been in Shipley's time, but with the fine panelling and carved chimney mantels of the interior barely visible beneath modern decoration and partitioning. It is now the head office of the Maidstone and District Motor Services Company,[17] and what was once a two-acre garden has been covered with motor-bus garages. Many of the other Georgian houses of Knightrider Street have been completely destroyed, yet it is still possible to imagine the street when it was the background of Shipley's busy 'retirement', and saw him endeavouring to divide the day in the manner of the 'great Secretaries of State . . . and the late King of Prussia of Glorious Memory' by means of a time-table written on a slate and displayed in his workroom.[18] There he would carry out his electrical and chemical experiments which were sometimes interrupted by 'so much company, in the holiday season,[19] cure his chagrin, like Montesquieu, by 'an Hour of reading',[18] correspond with the Society of Arts in London, and write the minutes and keep the accounts of the Maidstone Society.

The Maidstone Society for Promoting Useful Knowledge

was said in 1786 to have been established 'for some time past'.[20] In that year, as will be seen, it was refounded by Shipley as a Society for the whole of Kent. But the date of its original foundation and the part Shipley played therein cannot at present be determined. It may even have existed before Shipley came to Maidstone or been started by someone else after his arrival. However, the earliest evidence for its existence is dated 1783, when Shipley was playing an important part in its proceedings. Therefore it is quite likely that, as J. M. Russell suggested, Shipley himself founded it soon after he settled in the town.[21]

The membership of the Maidstone Society was drawn, like that of the Society of Arts, from the 'Nobility, Clergy, Gentlemen, Merchants and Tradesmen'.[20] By 1786, on the eve of its expansion into a county society, it numbered forty subscribing and twenty-nine corresponding members. The associations with Shipley, who held the office of Treasurer, and with the Society of Arts, were very strong. Lord Romney was the common President of both Societies, and his son, Charles Marsham, was among four other subscribing members of the Maidstone Society who also belonged to the Society of Arts.[22] Benjamin Franklin, Alexander Garden and Arthur Young, all members of the Society of Arts and friends of Shipley, were corresponding members of the Maidstone Society, as were George Cockings and Richard Samuel, respectively the Register and Assistant Secretary of the Society of Arts. Shipley's nephew and namesake, the Dean of St. Asaph, his nephew-in-law, Sir William Jones, and his former pupil, Richard Cosway, were also corresponding members. Under Shipley's influence, the Maidstone Society seems to have copied its procedure from the Society of Arts.

Bound up in a memorandum book which Shipley used for making rough notes during his time as Register of the London Society and which he added to in later years, is a printed copy of the 'Rules and Orders' of the London Society amended by Shipley to suit the Maidstone Society. The amendments take the form of pencil markings meaning either the inclusion or the retention of the particular passages, but certainly suggesting an overall similarity between the procedures of the two Societies, which is confirmed by some notes in the same book which Shipley made for a meeting of the Maidstone Society. As would have been the case for a meeting of the London Society, Shipley referred to the consideration of premiums, to the business of Committees and to the reading of 'the last minutes'. The minutes have not been preserved, yet it is significant in itself that Shipley should have used this same memorandum book for his work with both societies.[18]

He brought to bear on his Maidstone scheme the full weight of his prestige as the honoured founder of the Society of Arts. The public recognition which the London Society gave him in the 1780s gained him 'much credit' in Kent and made him determined 'to stir up as many as I can of our Principal Landed Gentlemen to carry into execution in a very extensive manner any of those Useful improvements in Agriculture which have been brought to light under your [i.e. the London Society's] Patronage'.[23]

The Maidstone Society's most spectacular achievement was its fight against a violent outbreak of fever which took place at the County Gaol in 1783. Fifteen fatal cases were reported and fifty-five other prisoners were infected. A Committee of the Society was appointed to raise funds to assist the sick prisoners and to pay for equipment to be used in fighting the epidemic. Lord Romney gave a supply of 'Thieves' vinegar' which produced 'most salutary effects . . . in correcting the infectious air in the wards of the prison'. The Prison Surgeon, Thomas Day, installed on the Society's behalf lime-water showers for the same purpose and, to quote from the Society's *Transactions*, 'Mr. Shipley, at the same time invented several instruments, one to fumigate the infected air, others to correct the putrid air breathed in the wards, while several alterations were ordered by the medical gentlemen of the Society, who attended at the gaol, and with the utmost benevolence, contributed their aid in defeating the horrid contagion that raged therein'. The Grand Jury and Judge of Assize gave 'public thanks' to the Society for its services in this instance.[24]

The 'principal intentions' of the Maidstone Society were 'to promote improvements in agriculture in all its branches',[20] but no account of its work in this sphere has survived. However, in a letter he wrote to Arthur Young in 1785, Shipley referred to the Maidstone Society's 'Desiderata', 'many of whom [sic] we have introduced here',[25] and it is reasonable to assume that these were the items he printed in 1786 as:

Cattle, new and useful sorts to introduce, also of sheep and swine.

Poultry, new and useful breeds.

Fruit trees for orchards, new and valuable sorts.

Seeds and plants for gardens, new and useful sorts.

Implements in husbandry and gardening, new and useful sorts.

Manures, new and useful sorts.[20]

The Maidstone Society probably took an interest in all these matters, and it is certain that Shipley was active in at least two of them. He devised his own 'new and useful' implements for gardening and orchard cultivation, as can be seen from his communications to the Society of Arts in 1786.[26] His letter to Arthur Young concluded with a promise: 'Sometime in October next I intend to send you a Collection of Cuttings of the large Lancashire Walnut Gooseberries, they are of a Monstrous Size and have a very delicious taste, and I hope they will please.'[25]

Yet if his years in Kent, where agricultural improvements had been carried on 'for several ages past',[20] stimulated Shipley to practise husbandry, they did not see the end of the exercise of his old skill in the 'polite arts'. In 1786 he produced to the Maidstone Society 'two instruments of his own contrivance; one for measuring all the proportions of the perpendicular heights of buildings that are inaccessible, the other for taking perspective views of landscapes, or views of the sea coasts from on board a ship, which may be found very useful to voyagers on discovery'. He also drew and painted for his own amusement. Sixty drawings by him of old and interesting buildings at Maidstone were listed as being in existence in the last century; unfortunately, like so much other evidence of his skill as an artist, they seem to have been either lost or destroyed.[27]

Seventeen-eighty-six was also the year in which Shipley undertook the expansion of the Maidstone Society's work to cover the whole of Kent. In March he told the London Society that 'the Form of a fund is drawn up and ready to be printed, and with several other Gentlemen I have procured . . . Letters of Recommendation to many of our principal Landed Gentlemen, and we are to wait on them with Invitations . . . to join us'.[23] By the end of the year he had published his *Proposal to Establish a Society for Promoting Useful Knowledge in the County of Kent*,[20] which was the 'Form of a fund' he had mentioned. He included it in the 'Desiderata' already quoted, a list of the sixty-nine members of the Maidstone Society, and an eloquent preamble of more than a thousand words. This contained many echoes of his earlier pamphlets and shows that his faith in 'Improvement' remained as great as ever after three decades. He referred first to 'the generous design of that truly patriotic institution the Society of Arts; whose views extend over the whole British Empire', and which had acted as an inspiration to 'similar Associations upon a more limited plan'. Then after mentioning the achievements of various county societies, he listed some of the endeavours of the Maidstone Society and concluded with an appeal to Kentish patriotism, which shows how well he understood the economy of that county. Part of this conclusion ran as follows:

The inhabitants of the county of Kent have been the greatest improvers of agriculture of any others in this kingdom. They first introduced the cultivation of apples, cherries and hops; sainfoin, lucerne, and some other valuable grasses amongst us; and by their ingenuity and public spirit the woollen, silk, paper, thread, and some other valuable manufactures were first established, amongst us; and this nation is greatly indebted to them for the eminent services they have done to their country by the improvements they have made in various other branches of useful knowledge. This county is better formed by nature than perhaps any other in the kingdom for such an institution, not only on account of its nearness to the metropolis, but also for the great conveniencies it has for sending heavy or bulky goods to London by water, as it is more than two parts in three surrounded by the sea and the Thames, has many navigable rivers, and there are but few places within the same from whence goods may not soon be carried to some port or navigable river, and sent to London by water; there is also in this county a very great variety of hill and vale, and a vast number of different soils, most of which are capable of being much improved. Therefore as a proposal is now made, which, if properly encouraged will be a means of diffusing beneficial knowledge, method and custom to every part of this province, it is not to be doubted, but the inhabitants, in general, will be as ready to *cultivate* useful knowledge amongst them, as their forefathers have been in former ages assiduous to *plant* it.

Shipley, though seventy-one years of age, was still willing to undertake an arduous canvass, 'thinking it inglorious' to remain inactive in the face of public need and opportunity.

[xiv] *More Inventions, 1778–87*

As would be expected, Shipley's move to Maidstone in 1768 meant a decline in the number of his attendances at the Committees of the Society of Arts. Between April 1768 and March 1781 his presence is recorded only twice in the Committee Minute Books. On 28th April 1772, he attended the Committee of Mechanics in company with Benjamin Franklin and took part in the consideration of improvements of 'Wheel carriages'. He was again in London 24th April 1776 to deliver an account of his floating light to a meeting of the whole Society, but did not attend any Committees. On 19th November 1778 he was present at the Committee of Mechanics for one of the trials of his coal-burning method, though as will shortly be seen, he carried on most of the arrangements for these trials by post from Maidstone. Then in 1781 he began what might be called his second period as a frequent attender, which was to last until 1787; during these years he was present at twenty-five meetings of Committees. His annual totals for the various Committees—Agriculture, Chemistry, Manufactures, Mechanics, Miscellaneous, and Polite Arts—are shown in the following table:

	Agric.	*Chem.*	*Manuf.*	*Mech.*	*Misc.*	*Pte. Art*
1781	0	0	0	4	0	1
1782	1	0	0	1	1	1
1783	0	0	0	0	2	0
1784	0	0	0	0	0	0
1785	0	0	0	0	0	0
1786	2	1	0	3	0	0
1787	1	0	1	3	1	2

With all his Maidstone preoccupations it is unlikely that his attendances for this later period would have equalled those for 1760–8, when it may be remembered he attended at Committees 151 times. His interests continued to embrace the whole range of the Society's work, but his presence at Committee meetings can usually be linked with certain specific proposals of his own. His educational schemes, which will be considered in a later section, caused him to attend the Committees of Polite Arts and Agriculture in 1781, 1782, 1786 and 1787. He submitted tools to the Committee of Mechanics in the same years; these will be described below. But first of all something must be said of two 'economical' proposals which he laid before the Society at this time.

On 9th November 1778 Shipley wrote to Samuel More, the Society's Secretary, saying that he proposed 'to come to London next week' and asking More to mention to the Society's meeting, 'on Wednesday next', a 'method of burning Sea Coal to a much greater advantage than by the usual methods in Stoves and Grates' which he (Shipley) would be willing to demonstrate 'to any Committee who will meet after Wednesday se'nt the 18th instant'.[1] 'The making Fires and burning Fuel to the greatest advantage have often employed the thoughts of some of our most eminent men, as Boyle, Boerhave, Desaguliers, Shaw, Hales and many others', wrote Shipley in a subsequent letter.[2] To his list could now be added Rumford and numerous nineteenth-century experimenters.[3] The problem has, indeed, been of frequent public interest in the present century. The hardships which could result from excessive coal prices were familiar to Shipley from his Northampton days. In Maidstone in the late 1770s he found 'the dearness' of coal made it 'a very considerable article in Housekeeping' and he anticipated further price increases 'should this horrid war continue'.[4] His method, he claimed, would lead to 'a saving of more than one Fourth of the Expense of Coals' and was already used 'to advantage' by 'several of my friends at Maidstone'; and he thought that it might have a use beyond the domestic sphere:

> I suppose that such a fire may serve to dry Malt and Hops, and for many other valuable Purposes in many different Arts and Manufactories, but should this my Proposal be not found to answer what I suppose it may for such valuable Purposes, yet my wife and family are very certain of this, that such a bright fire without Smoke is much more useful for many domestic Purposes, in cookery, as roasting, Boiling and broiling, than fires made in the common way where there is much smoke.[2]

Shipley believed he could reduce the smokiness of fires and prolong their burning time by feeding them at the bottom 'instead, as is common, at the top'. He inserted into grates 'a cross iron or T' which helped to keep in the smoke and he had designed a special shovel and a poker to be used for his feeding method.[5] A preliminary trial was made by the Society's Committee of Mechanics on 19th November 1778, when 'Mr. Shipley attending, explained his method', but there was no time to reach a decision on that occasion so arrangements were made for another trial which was to be held in the Society's Great Room. Shipley had to go back to Maidstone, but he supplied detailed instructions for the Committee's guidance in a letter which was almost two thousand words in length, and which indicated the beginning of an intense anxiety lest the success of the experiments should be endangered by the use of wrong materials or inaccurate observation so that 'perhaps at the end of the process you may think that I am in the wrong Grate'.[2]

His fears were justified, for the Committee spent from five minutes past eight until half past nine on the evening of 2nd December trying his method, but as he learnt from a friend, 'his method did not seem to have any advantage over the common method of burning Coals in the other Grate' and 'as the evening was very wet and the Gentlemen came late there was not time . . . to come to any resolution about its merits'. The Committee 'postponed further consideration till another trial be made'. Shipley believed that this experiment had failed because the coal which he 'ordered to be procured . . . spoiled my whole process'. 'This coal,'[6] he told Samuel More, 'on enquiry I find is the Marden[7] coal which is much used by the Blacksmiths, [it] . . . flames much at first, but the flame is soon over.'

At Maidstone he carried out some experiments of his own and found 'that two sorts of inflammable Coals answer the purpose exceeding well for feeding fires, viz, the Washington and the Harraton Coals[8] . . . I will very shortly send the Gentlemen an account of some particular trials I have made with these coals'.[9] He made this promise to More on 22nd December, but was 'prevented by a variety of company in the Holidays' from completing the minutes of these experiments in time for the third investigation which the Committee of Mechanics undertook on 14th January 1779. He was nevertheless able to ensure that the Committee used the 'Society's coals' instead of the unsatisfactory 'Marden' coal and to repeat his instructions in a letter which, though not written until the 13th, arrived in time for the meeting: 'Should this Experiment not succeed according to my expectations', he told the Committee, 'I don't doubt but when I come to London, which will be very soon, I shall be able then to show you an experiment of this kind which will give perfect satisfaction.'[10]

The Committee's experiment was described in the following minute:

Took into consideration the letters from Mr. Shipley on burning coals.

Read a letter from Mr. Shipley dated 13th instant.

Two fires having been lighted at 4 o'clock, the Committee directed the messenger to feed one of the fires according to the method proposed by Mr. Shipley and the other in the usual manner at 20 minutes past 7 o'clock.

At 50 minutes past 8, the two fires having been fed in the different manners with one quart of coals each,

Resolved the fire kept in the old way appears to be the brightest.

Resolved that the fire kept in Mr. Shipley's way promises to last longest.

Resolved that as Mr. Shipley in his letter mentions his intention of coming to town soon the further consideration of this business be postponed till he comes.[11]

After this reasonably satisfactory conclusion, Shipley does not seem to have bothered the Committee again with the matter, for there are no records of subsequent correspondence or experiments. A year later the Committee recommended that the Society should 'return thanks to Mr. Shipley for this communication',[12] and his long and anxious letters were bound up with other manuscripts recording the Society's 'Transactions' for 1779/80.

The Society's minutes for 31st January 1781 record the receipt of a letter from Shipley about 'a wheel barrow'. The letter has not been preserved, but the minutes of the Committee of Mechanics for March and April 1781 show that he attended meetings to test improvements in wheelbarrows which had been submitted by other inventors.[13] Unfortunately, there is no record of the nature of Shipley's interest in this subject. However, at the end of 1781 he wrote a letter to the Society 'on the use of tin foil for the purpose of laying between the Leathers of the Soles of Shoes',[14] which earned him a vote of thanks and was included in the MS. Transactions for 1781/2. The proposal was both practical and novel,[15] and was described by Shipley with his customary meticulousness:

Maidstone, 10th Dec. 1781

Gentlemen,

As business[16] frequently calls me from Home in wet weather I often find that if my Shoes are not very substantial and Proof against the weather I am very liable to catch cold, which cold I suppose was received at the Soles of the Feet as the Skin is there very thin and Poreous. Therefore I endeavoured to provide some substance which being put by the Shoemaker between the Soles of the Shoes when first made, might repel the moisture. I had then by me a Roll of Tin Foil for to make some Electrical Experiments, which I thought might probably answer my purpose as I knew that it was proof against water for a long Time; and as it was very light and ductile and might be purchased at a low price, I thought that this substance might probably answer the Purpose. And therefore I cut out of my Roll of Tin Foil, with a Pair of Scissors, a Piece for each Shoe large enough to cover the Sole of the Shoes as far as the Heel. I then ordered my Shoemaker to make me a pair of shoes, and put these pieces of Tin Foil between the Leathers in the Sole of each Shoe, and I found that the Tin Foil answered the purpose of keeping out the wet much better than I expected, for it not only kept my Feet very dry, but also very warm.

I have left with Mr. Cockings[17] a Roll of this Tin Foil for any Gentleman to have a Piece of it for each Shoe, that desires to try the Experiment with a Pair of New Shoes. The Tin Foil may be cut to fit the Soles of the Shoes thus: take a Piece of Paper and put one of the Shoes on it, then mark the shape of the Sole as far as the Heel with a Black lead Pencil on the Paper, cut the Paper according to the Blacklead lines with a pair of Scissors then cut the Tin Foil from this Paper which may be done without injuring the Tin Foil, care must be taken that it is not rumpled lest it crack. It may be put between the Leaves of a Book till it is delivered to the Shoemaker; it is very tough unless rumpled or folded. It is very cheap and will cost no more than 16 pence per pound. It may be had at Mr. Spackman's at No. 4 Jewry Street, Aldgate,[18] or at any of the Foil Beaters in other Streets.

I think that this method will be convenient for those Gentlemen who take long Walks when the Streets are wet, this Tin Foil will keep out the Dew which scarce any leather be it never so well seasoned will do. The expense of the Foil will be about one Penny for a Pair of Shoes. I am Gentlemen,

Your very Humble Servant,
W. SHIPLEY[19]

A year later, in December 1782, Shipley was present at meetings of the Committees of Agriculture and Mechanics.[20] He did not, however, submit proposals for their consideration, although he was at that time engaged in discussion of an educational scheme with the Committee of Polite Arts. In April 1783 he was present at two meetings of the Miscellaneous Matters Committee, but had no specific proposals to make. Then, after an interval of non-attendance lasting nearly three years, he was again at meetings of the Committee of Agriculture on 30th January and 6th February 1786, and on 16th and 23rd February at the Committee of Mechanics. The latter Committee had already shown its appreciation on 9th February for the first of a number of devices and instruments which Shipley was to present to the Society in 1786. It was a 'Bolt and Nail Drawer', which the Committee resolved to be 'a Simple and powerful Instrument for the purposes intended'.[21] On 22nd May, the Committee of Agriculture noted the gift of 'an Implement or Tool for Gardening or Husbandry presented by Mr. Shipley . . . which consists of a spear pointed bar fixed to a Spade Handle, with a side Iron projecting for the foot to rest on to force the spear point into the earth'. Four days afterwards the Committee of Mechanics considered 'several Garden Tools, presented to the Society by Mr. Shipley'. The minutes listed them as:

> Two of the Tools are somewhat similar to a pickaxe, but one End is a Chisel or flat cutting Edge, instead of a point, these are of different sizes.
>
> A small Tin Shovel with the Handle placed nearly upright so that the Bottom of the Shovel rests flat on the Ground for any Weeds or loose Gravel . . . [to] be swept into it by a small broom.
>
> A small Hoe having a small rake fixed on the opposite side.

Shipley was present at the meeting and he arranged to supply 'a more particular Description of these Tools'.[22] This he provided in the February of the following year, 1787,[23] when he was again attending meetings connected with his educational schemes. On 1st February 1787 the Committee of Mechanics heard him speak and

> Resolved it is the opinion of the Committee that the Tools presented by Mr. Shipley are designed for the use of Ladies and Gentlemen who may be disposed to amuse themselves in Gardening [and] are well adapted to that purpose.
>
> Resolved to recommend to the Society to accept this Present and to return Thanks to Mr. Shipley for the same.

Gardening as a recreation and estate management in miniature were to have a place in the schemes for educational reform which Shipley also presented to the Society in the 1780s.

[xv] *Educational Schemes, 1781–7*

During the years 1781 to 1787, when Shipley was demon-
strating his inventions in household economy and gardening
to the Society of Arts, he was also endeavouring to engage the
Society's interest in a scheme for national educational reform.
His own interest in educational matters was deep-rooted and
arose naturally from his former profession as an art teacher and
his life's work as a philanthropist. He had studied Locke's
celebrated treatise and was conversant both with the long-
standing 'Grand Tour' controversy and with the workings of
the Charity School system.[1] At Northampton in the 1740s he
had known Doddridge's famous Academy and had probably
seen the school for poor children which that eminent educa-
tionist also conducted.[2] With Priestley, Hanway and Raikes he
was a fellow 'honorary and corresponding member' of the
Odiham Society and in 1786, when that Society was encouraging Sunday Schools, he sent it his own plans for educating the poor.[3] In his printed scheme of 1753 for the foundation of a Society of Arts, he had advocated the giving of
premiums 'for improvements in the present plans of education'
and in 1786 he was to include a similar proposal in his plan for
the expanded Maidstone Society.[4] 'The culture of vegetables,
Plants, Trees and Cattle' was, in his mind, of the utmost importance, but he believed that the 'culture of youth', in an
analogy he loved to draw, was even more important, for, as he
told the Society of Arts in 1782, 'I believe it may with the
greatest truth be affirmed that the great or contemptible
Figures, which various nations have made in all ages, have been
chiefly owing to the good or bad plans which they have
adopted for the Education of their youth.'[1]

Shipley wished the Society to give premiums to schools and
academies which adopted a method of teaching languages
through conversation. He believed that this method was much

quicker than the 'grammatical' system generally employed in his period and he hoped that the time 'saved to youth in learning languages expeditiously' would be 'employed in learning various Arts . . . which are rarely taught in schools or academies'.[1] He first laid what he called his 'Proposal for Improving the present plans for the Education of Youth used in this Kingdom' before the Society in February 1781. The Society's Committee of Polite Arts, meeting on 10th March with Shipley present, found the proposal 'deserving the encouragement of the Society',[5] but, as Shipley himself related, 'when the report of the said Committee was read at the next meeting of the Society, the Gentlemen were divided in their Opinions concerning the proposal being within the Plan of the Society, and on putting the question the votes were equal. And Mr. Hooper,[6] who was in the Chair . . . expressed some little uneasiness about the Question being decided by his single vote, I therefore agreed to have the Question postponed.' Shipley waited until the end of the next year before broaching the subject again, and by that time he had 'improved his former proposal'. On 25th November 1782 he wrote a 5,000-word letter to the Society which, because it had more success than his previous communication, has been preserved in the manuscript Transactions.[1] Like his letters on coal economy, it rambles and digresses in a manner attributable to his advanced age, and is better summarised than quoted in full.

After recalling the reasons for the Society's postponement of his proposal, Shipley said that he had now revised it and that he believed it 'does exactly come within the true meaning and spirit of the plan of our Society'. He then described his method of teaching Latin. A competent Usher would 'select a few of his pupils who have the greatest memories and the best flow of words, and instead of learning the Classical authors, they may learn by heart Dialogues in familiar phrases in Latin and English'. The recitation of these dialogues would spread throughout the school and 'by discoursing together' all the boys would 'soon learn the true meaning of a number of phrases proper to be used in common Discourse and . . . to ask a few questions and discourse a little without learning their Parts by Heart'. 'After that,' continued Shipley:

> the Plays of Terence and Plautus may be read in the school by the same young gentlemen in manner following, viz. the best English Translations of those authors for the Purpose may be procured, and one of the Scholars who reads very well may be employed to read one of the Acts . . . in English, while all the rest of them sit by with their Latin originals, and observe very minutely every expression,; and another boy who reads very well may also take a Latin original . . . and read the same Act in Latin, while the rest of his companions are there with their English Translations, and take notice of every passage very attentively and thus they may in the same manner go through the whole Play; and in the process of time through the whole Book; by which means they will soon learn a great number of Latin phrases from Authors who writ the Latin language in its greatest purity; and after they have proceeded in this manner for sometime, they may begin to form discourses somewhat like the Dialogues of the familiar forms of speaking above mentioned and thus they may introduce into their Discourses the same kind of Phrases which they met with in Plautus' and Terence's Plays, and make such Phrases their own.

Shipley mentioned other Latin works which could be studied in the same way and concluded by suggesting that the boys might

> use some of the same gymnastic Games, and exercises which were used by Youths amongst the old Romans and Greeks;

as shooting with bows and arrows, darting the Javelin, tossing the Quoit, Rowing, swimming, &c. all which will much enlarge the Discourses in Latin of some of the Bye-standers; and they will thus improve themselves ten times faster in the learning the Latin Language while these Games are performing, than Youth[s] generally do in schools where they learn Latin in the old way by grammar rules.

Modern languages, Shipley believed, could be taught in the same way. He had himself learnt French by conversation 'without any of that laborious application which I had used at school in learning Latin'.[7] He therefore proposed that Italian, Spanish, French and High Dutch should be taught in schools in the same manner as he had 'proposed for Latin'; an increased knowledge of these languages amongst Britons would be 'very beneficial to the Public' by 'promoting trade'. But this was not the core of his proposal. He believed that it would do little good unless 'articles of importance for Youth to know in future life may be taught them . . . in the time that is saved . . . by teaching languages expeditiously by my proposed method'. The first of these articles was to be 'the teaching of virtue . . . without which I suppose that the more knowledge men have it will be always so much the worse'. Then came the 'various branches of Experimental Philosophy, Lectures in Astronomy, Geography, Optics, Mechanics, Hydrostatics, Pneumatics, also lectures and experiments in Agriculture, Planting, Gardening, management of apiaries, draining of lands, Breeding of Cattle, and other such rural Amusements; also, Merchants accounts . . . Drawing, Perspective and Shorthand'. He digressed at length on the value of inculcating moral precepts from the Scriptures and from selected classical and modern authors, and gave a programme for the 'Tour through Great Britain' which he believed was useful in itself and also a 'very proper preparation' for the 'Tour of Europe'. Agriculture, he believed, could be taught by means of experiments on miniature estates in which fields would be represented by beds 16 ft. square.

In such Beds Experiments in growing any sort of Grain, and also for the manuring them may be made; with as much or perhaps more certainty than in the large fields; the Land may be ploughed and harrowed in the common way, and some of the lightest part of the culture may be done by the young Gentlemen as part of their Gymnastic Exercises; also the planting of various sorts of Timber Trees, and under-woods may be taught both in the Theory and Practice; and young Gentlemen from their Childhood may be taught these things; which kind of Knowledge may often be of the greatest Service to those Gentlemen, who have Estates.

When these properly educated and travelled young gentle-men grew up and took their places in the Houses of Parliament they might be expected to serve 'the Intentions of the Society of Arts', and Shipley thought that the Society might itself gain members by sponsoring 'plans of education'. Here he had in mind the decline in the numbers of members which had been observable since 1770[8] and he recalled the time when the Society's chief work had been the judging of art awards 'which were esteemed both useful and entertaining by great numbers of gentlemen', and when, as he remembered, 'twenty to thirty new members [were] ballotted for in an evening . . . had we not patronised these very entertaining and extensive subjects . . . this Society of Arts had not now existed. The proposal before you is much more extensive and useful than the Polite Arts proposal and will, I believe, to many be no less enter-taining.'

'Every class of youth' including the poor, wrote Shipley, could have their education improved 'if they were taught to learn by Heart such Lessons of Morality and Virtue, suitable to their Station', and he offered to supply the Society with the plans of 'working Charity Schools such as [he had] seen in the counties of Norfolk and Suffolk'. His letter ended with a quotation from Pope and an appeal to Royal examples:

These are Imperial Works and worthy Kings[9]
Such undertakings are so truly great that they have often engaged the thoughts of some of our Kings and Queens, as King Alfred, Henry the 6th, Henry the 8th, Edward the 6th, Queen Elizabeth and some others, besides these Great Personages; some monarchs of other Nations have gained more real and deserved honours by civilising their own people by proper plans of Education, than . . . any other Monarchs whatever have done by their far extended Conquests: from such Monarchs among the ancients we may select Cyrus the Great, and amongst the moderns, we may rank Peter the Great, Tsar of Muscovy. By what has been said you may perceive Gentlemen of what very great importance your encouraging useful Plans of Education may be to this Nation, and I can conclude with wishing all possible Success to every Article which you have Patronised, for the benefit of the public, and am

Gentlemen,

your very humble Servant,

W. SHIPLEY

Shipley attended the Committee of Polite Arts on 10th December, when a report in favour of his proposal was again submitted to the Society—and on 18th he had the satisfaction of learning that premiums were to be offered for language teaching. The Society published the following advertisement in the newspapers and had 500 copies printed for distribution amongst headmasters:[10]

To the Masters of Academies or Schools

TEACHING LANGUAGES

Whereas it has been observed that the living languages, or languages spoken in schools, are much sooner acquired than the dead languages, which are only taught grammatically.

The Society, desirous to improve the present mode of education, hereby offer the gold medal to the master of any academy, or school for boys, situated within, or not more than thirty miles distant from London, who shall within three years, from the date of this advertisement, teach the greatest number of scholars, not less than four, to write and to speak Latin, in common conversation, correctly and fluently.

Also, the gold medal for teaching in the like manner, each of the following languages, viz. the German, the Spanish, and the Italian, being commercial languages, not usually taught at schools in England.

The masters who propose to be candidates for the above premiums, are to send notice of their intention to claim them, to the Society, at their house in the Adelphi, on or before the second Tuesday in November, 1786. Soon after which, the Society will appoint a day for examining the young gentlemen, and for adjudging the said claims.

And in order to encourage assiduity in the scholars, whose masters apply for the above premiums, the Society will give to the greatest proficient in each of the said languages, the silver medal.

N.B. Any information for the further improvement of the education of youth, in languages, will be thankfully received.

The offer of this premium was repeated each year until 1786, when Dr. James Egan of Greenwich successfully demonstrated the prowess of his pupils in conversational Latin.[11]

Shipley had been unable to accept an invitation to attend the judging—which certainly fulfilled his prophecy regarding the entertainment value of education[12]—but was in London a month later with proposals for another premium based on his 1782 communication. At a Society meeting held on 31st January 1787 a motion to award a premium to the masters of academies and schools for boys, 'who shall introduce into his plan of education a knowledge of the theory and practices of agriculture', was referred to the Committee of Agriculture. No name is attached to the motion in the minutes but there can be little doubt that Shipley was behind it, as he was present when it came before the Committee on 5th February. The Committee drafted an advertisement:

> The Gold Medal will be given to the Master of any Academy or school within thirty miles of London who shall qualify the greatest number of youths not fewer than four in the knowledge of the theory and practice of Agriculture and Gardening.
>
> And the Silver Medal will be given to that youth who shall have made the greatest progress in these Arts.
>
> It is expected that a Journal of the young Gentlemen's proceedings be kept and that they submit to an examination on the subject.
>
> The Masters who propose to be Candidates for the above premiums are to signify their intention to the Society at their House in the Adelphi on or before the second Tuesday in November 1791 soon after which the Society will appoint a day for the examination of the Pupils.

However, the Society's meeting of 7th February refused to adopt the Committee's suggestion, so nothing came of this part of Shipley's proposal. Similarly the Polite Arts Committee, which wished to renew the premiums for language teaching and heard Shipley urge their extension to scholastic boarding houses on 2nd February, had its intention thwarted by the Society on 4th April. Nor did the Society appear to show interest in Shipley's suggestion about the importance of educating the poor. Yet with a curious prescience he had anticipated what were to be its principal activities in the 1850s. At the opening of the Society's Hundredth Session in 1853, Harry Chester, founder of the Society's Examinations System and then Chairman of the Council, was to announce 'that an improved education for the whole people, rich and poor, adult and child, is the first requisite for the improvement of manufactures, commerce and the arts; that a liberal measure of science must enter into that education; and that it is the duty of this Society to promote vigorously this great object'.[13]

Seventeen-eighty-seven was to be the last year in which Shipley would attend meetings of the Society's Committees. He may have been disappointed at the lack of response to his educational schemes, but a more likely explanation could be found in the pressure of his work away from London caused by the expansion of the Maidstone Society. It should also be remembered that he was now in his seventies and could hardly be expected to make many more journeys from home. He was, however, up in London again in May 1787, when his last recorded attendances at Committee meetings took place—on 17th May, at the Committee of Mechanics, and on 21st May at the Committee of Manufactures. In both cases he had no special communication to deliver and was simply exercising his right as a member to attend. But on the 21st, in the absence of both chairmen, he conducted the meeting and thus ended his long years of service by presiding over the proceedings of a Committee of the Society of Arts. In another sense he was to preside at many future Committee meetings, for in August 1787 his portrait by Cosway was placed above the chimney in the Committee Room at the Society's House in the Adelphi.

A new frame and inscription were ordered, proclaiming once again that 'his public spirit gave rise to this Society'.[14]

[xvi] The closing years, 1788–1803

The Kentish Society for Promoting Useful Knowledge was especially active in 1788. It attempted a geological survey of the County, continued with its encouragement of the various branches of agriculture and patronised a number of inventions.[1] In spite of his age, Shipley remained busy in the Society's affairs. A letter exists from him to Sir Joseph Banks which is dated 2nd February 1788, and is signed 'William Shipley, Treasurer to the [Kentish] Society',[2] and there are notes in his Memorandum Book showing he was at work for the Society later in the year. Soon after, however, the Society was disturbed by some sort of rift amongst its members. Sir William Jones, Shipley's nephew-in-law, wrote to him from India in September 1788, lamenting 'the sad effects of party, or rather faction in your Maidstone Society, but hope (to use a word of Dr. Johnson) that it will redintegrate'.[3] No details of this dispute are known, but it may have been the cause of the falling off in attendances at the Society's meetings which Shipley deplored in an undated printed circular to the members[4] and which was to lead after five years to its dissolution and to the establishment of a new society with more limited objectives.

As Shipley would have found through his experience at the Society of Arts, differences of opinion over scientific and artistic matters could be as heated as those over government and religion. And although it was always possible for these greater issues to exacerbate the tempers of the virtuosi, it need not be supposed that the members of the Kentish Society were divided over Church and State. Nevertheless, Shipley's family connections with such controversial figures as Sir William Jones may not have gone unnoticed in this connection; and no account of his life would be complete without some attempt to assess his own standing in regard to national politics and religion.

Shipley's brother had been known as an outspoken Whig ever since his election to the Episcopal Bench in 1769. An intimate friend of Benjamin Franklin, he opposed the American war almost to the point of disloyalty. 'Princes,' he said, 'are the trustees, not the proprietors of the people.' In 1783 Dean Shipley, the Bishop's son, was prosecuted for publishing Sir William Jones's radical dialogue on the *Principles of Government*, which contained a similar criticism of the royal power.[5] But Jones used to modify his views to humour his friend Samuel Johnson, and he wished Lord Thurlow to be assured that 'I am no more a Republican than a Mahometan or a Gentoo'.[6] His letters to William Shipley are concerned with such neutral matters as the work of the Asiatic Society and with family news, and certainly do not make his correspondent appear a politician.[7]

Like all his brother's family, William Shipley knew Benjamin Franklin, but his acquaintance with the great American was based on a mutual interest in promoting useful knowledge.[8] It certainly survived what he once called the 'horrid war',[9] but so did his friendship with Alexander Garden, the distinguished botanist of South Carolina who had sided with the Crown during the revolution.[10] Shipley probably deplored the suffering caused to both sides by the conflict. He belonged, however, to the non-political world of scientists and philosophers. As a bishop, his brother Jonathan was expected to express opinions on matters of State. William, on the other hand, needed to be silent on such controversies, in order to unite—as he did when he founded the Society of Arts—Whigs and Tories, Churchmen and Dissenters, to work together for the public good. In the same way he made no public avowal of his religious beliefs, beyond insisting on the value of the Scriptures in his educational scheme. He had strong family ties with the established Church, yet he had been a close friend of Dr. Doddridge in Northampton and in Maidstone he was associated with the Rev. William Hazlitt, the Unitarian minister.[11]

William Shipley had no stake in the struggles of sects and parties. Joseph Moser called him 'one of the most loyal, benevolent, and inoffensive beings upon earth',[12] and Sir William Jones wrote of 'the pleasure of doing good' as the only reward he had ever sought.[13] In old age Shipley copied out a maxim by Montesquieu which might have served for his own:

> I easily pardon because I cannot hate,
> Hatred to me appears painful.[14]

Jonathan Shipley died at the end of 1788[15] and early the following year one of his servants arrived at Maidstone with a German communication which 'treated on some Branches of very useful knowledge', and had clearly been intended for his late master's brother. William forwarded it to the Society of Arts, and his accompanying letter, dated the 3rd February 1789, which was to be the last he would write to the Society, suggests through the irregularity of its handwriting that old age and possibly illness were also overtaking him.[16] Some type of physical ailment certainly affected him during the course of 1789 or early in 1790, for Sir William Jones, acknowledging in October 1790 'kind letters' from him which had arrived by ship in India, wrote: 'You are I hope quite recovered from your illness, and again promoting the welfare and convenience of mankind by your judicious exertions and ingenious inventions.'[13] Shipley's recovery was sufficient to enable him to accept election as a Fellow of the Linnean Society of London in 1792, and in 1795 to serve on the governing Committee of the reformed Kentish Society 'to promote Improvement in Agriculture, encourage Industry, and reward merit'. But by that time he was approaching eighty years of age and in 1796 he resigned from the Linnean Society, 'having scarce been in London since that time [his election]'.[17] The new Kentish Society did not survive its inaugural meetings[18] and Shipley probably retired from public activity during the last eight years of his life.

To the art world in London he was already something of a legend. Joseph Farington noted with interest in his diary for January 1794 the fact that Shipley was still alive.[19] In the *Memoirs* he completed in 1798, Thomas Jones recalled with affection the eccentricities of his old teacher, whom he believed had once made 'a serious proposal', in regard to the Foundling Hospital, 'that the whole Seminary should be converted into an Academy of Art, and all the Foundlings brought up Painters'.[20] Joseph Moser's story of Shipley's arrest as a suspected Jesuit has already been quoted and reference has been made to the sketch of Shipley's character from which it was taken. The *European Magazine* published Moser's sketch, which has much of the air of an obituary, in September 1803, although Shipley did not die until the end of that year. Moser gives a vivid description of Shipley's manner and appearance, confirming the impressions conveyed in the portraits by Cosway, Barry and Hincks:

WILLIAM SHIPLEY, ESQ.

This gentleman, who was the original projector of that laudable national institution, the Society for the Encouragement of Arts, Manufactures and Commerce, was, I have been informed, brother to Dr. Shipley, late Bishop of St. Asaph.

I remember him well; and as I never think of his talents and his services to the country, I might say to the world, but with esteem and veneration, I am therefore desirous of preserving a few traits of a character from whom the public has derived such incalculable advantages.

Mr. Shipley had, in early youth, among many other more abstruse researches, studied drawing. Whether he ever practised professionally as a painter, I am unable to say, but of his great merit as a drawing master, several very eminent artists that were his pupils, are still living instances. He was a man grave in his deportment, slow, and sometimes hesitating, in his speech, not from defects, but from consideration; and had, especially when sitting, something of the heavy appearance of the late Dr. Johnson, yet under this unpromising aspect, he possessed a most benevolent heart, joined to an inquisitive, intelligent, and highly cultivated mind. When he contemplated the plan of that Society which he afterwards formed and matured, I have known him sit for hours by the late Keeper of the Royal Academy . . . and with a loquacity unusual to him, discuss the rise and progress of, and the improvement that had been and might be made, in a variety of arts and manufactures. . . .

In mixed company, as I have hinted, Mr. Shipley was reserved, distant, and indeed silent to an extreme. When I have considered his manner, it has always brought to my mind the *Spectator*'s description of himself.[21]

The year 1804 was to see the fiftieth anniversary of the foundation of the Society of Arts, and in planning the celebrations well in advance, the Society arranged as early as February 1803 'that some particular Mark of Attention should be paid to Mr. Shipley the Founder', on the day of the distribution of premiums in the jubilee year.[22] At the 1803 distribution, which was held on 1st July, Dr. Charles Taylor, Secretary of the Society, spoke what the *Monthly Magazine* called 'a handsome tribute of respect to Mr. Shipley',[23] but before the projected anniversary celebration came round death had claimed the Founder of the Society. How far infirmity and old age clouded his mind at the last may not be determined, but it is to be hoped that he drew some comfort from this recognition, even though his retiring nature would have made him shrink from public participation in the intended ceremonies. He died in Maidstone at the close of the year[24] and was buried in the churchyard of All Saints. A simple monument commemorates his life and work:

To the memory of
WILLIAM SHIPLEY ESQ
late of this town
whose public Spirit
gave rise to the Society
established in London
for the Encouragement
of Arts, Manufactures
and Commerce
Ob 28 December, 1803 AET 89

B.M. = British Muesum
D.N.B. = *Dictionary of National Biography*
G.B. = Guard Books of the Society of Arts
Hudson and Luckhurst = D. Hudson and K. W. Luckhurst, *The Royal Society of Arts, 1754–1954* (London, 1954)
L.A. = Loose Archives of the Society of Arts
M.M. = Maidstone Museum and Art Gallery
Min. Com. = Minutes of Committees of the Society of Arts. (Names of the Committees being abbreviated as Ag. = Agriculture, Chem. = Chemistry, Man. = Manufactures, Mech. = Mechanics, Misc. = Miscellaneous Matters, P.A. = Polite Arts)
R.A. = Royal Academy
R.S.A. = Royal Society of Arts
Ryl. Eng. MSS. = English Manuscripts at the John Rylands Library, Manchester
Sub. Bks. = Subscription Books of the Society of Arts
Soc. Min. = Minutes of the Society of Arts
Trans. = Transactions of the Society of Arts
Trueman Wood = Sir H. T. Wood, *The History of the Royal Society of Arts* (London, 1913)

Note Page references cited as *p.* or *pp.* are to the present work. In all quotations from eighteenth-century MSS. spelling and punctuation has been modernised. Cross references in the notes and in part v of the bibliography cite chapter numbers in capital letters followed by the section number bracketed, e.g. TWO: (iii) refers to a note on chapter two, section iii.

NOTES

CHAPTER ONE

[a] The biographical problem

1 Trueman Wood, p. 7.

2 Hudson and Luckhurst, pp. 32–3.

3 See the 'Studies in the Society's Archives' (published at intervals in *Jnl. R.S.A.* since 1958), especially R. E. Schofield, 'The Society of Arts and the Lunar Society of Birmingham' (ibid., Vol. CVII, 1959, pp. 512–14, 668–71) and R. W. Allott, 'Joseph Bramah and his family as members of the Society, 1783–1845' (ibid., Vol. CVIII, 1960, pp. 62–5).

4 See *pp. 49–50.*

5 E. Robinson, 'The Profession of Civil Engineer in the Eighteenth Century: a portrait of Thomas Yeoman, F.R.S., 1704(?)–1781', *Annals of Science*, Vol. XVIII (4, 1962), p. 202.

6 See *pp. 33–8.*

7 The nineteenth-century home of the descendants of Bishop Jonathan Shipley (William's elder brother) who had moved from the original family residence, Twyford House (see *p. 22*).

8 E. Edwards, *Anecdotes of Painters* (London, 1808), p. xv; S. Redgrave, *Dictionary of Artists of the English School* (London, 1874), p. 374; M. Bryan, *Dictionary of Painters and Engravers* (London 1893, edit. R. E. Graves and W. Armstrong), Vol. II, p. 494.

9 M.M., MS. 'Lectures and Notes' by J. M. Allchin.

10 R.A., *Catalogue of Dutch Exhibition 1952–3*, no. 595.

11 Trueman Wood, p. 7.

12 U. Thieme and F. Becker, *Allgemeines Lexikon der Bildenden Kunstler*, Vol. XXX (Leipzig, 1936), p. 574; E. Bénézit, *Dictionnaire des Peintres* [etc.] (new edit. Paris, 1954), p. 743.

13 See *pp. 213–18.*

14 *The Houses of the Royal Society of Arts: a history and a guide* (London, 1966).

15 See *pp. 81–3.*

16 See *pp. 102, 231.*

17 See *pp. 201–7.*

18 See *pp. 42–6.*

[*b*] *The historical setting*

1 See *pp. 42–4.*

2 Part of the title of Andrew Yarranton's *England's Improvement by Sea and Land* (London, 1677).

3 See L. W. Hanson, *Contemporary Printed Sources for British and Irish Economic History, 1701–50* (Cambridge, 1963), pp. 854–9.

4 First published 1702.

5 See Vol. II, pp. 552–4, of Postlethwait's *Dictionary*.

6 Ibid., p. 639.

7 Ibid., Vol. I, Dedication.

8 See *pp. 43–4.*

9 See G. V. Portus, *Caritas Anglicana, or an historical enquiry into those religious and philanthropical societies that flourished in England between the years 1678 and 1740* (London, 1912), pp. 156–7.

10 See R. J. Allen, *The Clubs of Augustan London* (Cambridge, Mass., 1933), p. 129.

11 See T. Kelly, *George Birkbeck, pioneer of adult education* (Liverpool, 1957), p. 66.

12 'A Society of Gentlemen for the supporting mutual benevolence and their improvement in the Liberal

Sciences and Polite Learning', see J. Evans, *A History of the Society of Antiquaries* (Oxford, 1956), p. 54.

13 See Sir L. Cust, *History of the Society of Dilettanti* (London, 1898), p. 7.

14 See N. Hans, *New trends in education in the eighteenth century* (London, 1951), p. 159.

15 See J. Evans, op. cit., pp. 54–5.

16 See R. Bruce-Mitford, *The Society of Antiquaries of London; notes on its history and possessions* (London, 1951), p. 12.

17 See especially Sir H. Hartley, ed., *The Royal Society, its origin and founders* (London, 1960).

18 H. B. Wheatley, 'The Society of Arts', *Engineering*, Vol. LI (1891), pp. 83–6, quoted Trueman Wood, pp. 26–7. For Wheatley see Hudson and Luckhurst, pp. 361–2.

19 See *pp. 163–7*.

20 *Three Letters* [etc.], pp. 4–5.

21 See E. Bridgen, *A Short Account of the Great Benefits which have already risen to the Public, by means of the Society . . . of Arts* [etc.], (London, 1765), p. 5. A copy in manuscript of the *Three Letters* was made by Dr. Peter Templeman as part of his 'Historical Register' of the Society of Arts, compiled *cir.* 1760–9 (R.S.A., 'Dr. Templeman's Transactions', I, pp. 1–14).

22 *Three Letters*, pp. 6, 10.

23 Bridgen, loc. cit.

24 T. Sprat, *The History of the Royal Society of London for the Improving of Natural Knowledge* (London, 1667), p. 83. Later editions of Sprat appeared in 1722 and 1734. See the modern reprint edited by J. I. Cope and H. W. Jones (St. Louis and London, 1959), p. ix.

25 See Sprat, op. cit., Part II.

26　See D. Stimson, *Scientists and Amateurs* (London, 1949), pp. 91–4.

27　See *pp. 27–30*.

28　*The Tatler*, No. 221 (7th September 1710).

29　M.M., Letter from Edward Hughes to J. H. Allchin, *cir.* 1901.

30　See for example Horace Walpole on Hales (*Yale Edition of Horace Walpole's correspondence*, Vol. XX, London, 1960, p. 347) and 'Sir' John Hill on Baker (Hill, *A Review of the Works of the Royal Society*, London, 1715, passim).

31　See Thomas Shadwell's play *The Virtuoso* (1673), quoted by Stimson, op. cit., p. 93.

32　Dr. L. Trengrove of the University of Melbourne in his article 'Chemistry at the Royal Society in the Eighteenth Century, I', *Annals of Science*, Vol. 19 (1963/5), p. 183 et seq.

33　*Three Letters*, p. 9.

34　See *p. 168*.

35　See his pamphlet *Some Observations for Improvement of Trade by Establishing the Fishery of Great Britain* [etc.] (London, 1732).

36　See his letter to Sir Hans Sloane, 22nd June 1739, B.M., Sloane MSS. 4056, f. 60, and *The Best Mine above Ground* [etc.] (Dublin, 1742), p. i.

37　*The Best Mine above Ground*, pp. iv–v.

38　See B.M., loc. cit., 4056, f. 100.

39　Royal Society, Council Minutes, 20th October 1738.

40　See Trueman Wood, p. 243.

41　'Some also use premium in a synonymous sense with bounty', *A New Dictionary of Arts and Sciences* [etc.], Vol. III (London, 1754), p. 2528.

42　See W. Bowden, *Industrial Society in England Towards the the End of the Eighteenth Century* (New York, 1925),

p. 32–3; W. Cunningham, *The Growth of English Industry and Commerce in Modern Times* (Cambridge, 1903), Vol. I, p. 409.

43 See Trueman Wood, pp. 4–5; H. Hayward, *Thomas Johnson and English Rococo* (London, 1964), p. 23.

44 See *pp. 47–8*.

45 G.B. III, 119, Madden to Shipley, 26th November 1757.

46 See B. Williams, *The Whig Supremacy, 1714–60* (Oxford, 2nd ed., 1962, p. 340.

47 See *pp. 49–50*.

48 See Trueman Wood, pp. 28–46.

49 Charles Powell to Shipley, 1754 (G.B. I, 34).

50 Such as his friendship with George Michael Moser and his use of Old Slaughter's Coffee-House (see *pp. 26–7*). For Prince Frederick's Circle see M. Girouard, 'English Art and the Rococo', *Country Life*, Vol. CXXXIX (1966), p. 58 et seq.

51 J. Gwynn, *An Essay on Design* [etc.] (London, 1749), pp. 22, 26, 30, 31.

52 See F. Antal, *Hogarth and his place in European Art* (London, 1962), pp. 15–16.

53 See *p. 127*

54 L. Berchtold, *Essay to direct and extend the inquiries of Patriotic Travellers*, Vol. I (London, 1789), p. 372. The references are to John Howard, the prison reformer, Thomas Young, founder of the Philanthropic Society, and William Hawes, founder of the Humane Society.

55 See *p. 28*.

56 Quoted M. G. Jones, *The Charity School Movement* (Cambridge, 1938), p. 4.

CHAPTER TWO

[*i*] *Family background and education*

1   See article on William Shipley by Thomas Seccombe.

2   Trueman Wood, p. 9.

3   W. D. Bannerman, ed., *The Registers of St. Stephen Walbrook and of St. Benet, Sherehog, London*, Part I, Harleian Society Registers, Vol. XLIX (London, 1919), pp. 49, 50.

4   He was not alive in 1725/6 when William Davies made a will containing bequests in favour of his 'three grandchildren, viz. Jonathan, William and Martha Shipley'. (Original will of William Davies Gent. of Twyford, Hants., 10th February 1725/6, in the collection at Twyford Moors, and made available through the courtesy of Mrs. M. Dykes. Martha Shipley was born on 6th February 1717/18. See W. B. Bannerman, op cit., p. 127.)

5   His freedom was granted in July 1695, and he was apprenticed to Joshua Sharp for seven years from 10th November 1687 (information supplied by the City Chamberlain's Court).

6   Information relating to the monuments in Twyford Church kindly supplied by Miss K. M. R. Kenyon of Twyford.

7   See J. Nichols, *Literary Anecdotes of the Eighteenth Century* (London, 1812–15); Vol. VIII, p. 354.

8   Stationers' Company Records, 'Apprentices and Turnovers from April, 1728 to December, 1762', entry relating to the apprenticeship of Jonathan Shipley, Junior (quoted by kind permission of the Clerk to the Company).

9   See F. J. Froom, *A Site in the Poultry* (London, 1950), p. 90.

10   For the Trophy Tax levied on property owners in 1717, Jonathan Shipley's assessment was a little below the average (information kindly supplied by Mr. P. E. Jones of the City of London Record Office).

11   K. M. R. Kenyon, *Benjamin Franklin at Twyford* (Winchester, n.d.), p. 1; W. Page, ed., *Victoria History of the County of Hampshire*, Vol. III (London, 1908), p. 339.

12   This is speculation based on William Davies's will, which makes the size of his eldest daughter's inheritance subject to her being 'conformable' (Twyford Moors Collection).

13   His monument in Twyford Church gives the date of his death as 30th July 1719. The parish register records his burial on 3rd August (information kindly supplied by Miss K. M. R. Kenyon and the Archdeacon of Winchester).

14   Will of William Davies, 10th February 1725/6 (Twyford Moors collection). Davies died on 11th March 1726/7.

15   Stationers' Company Records, loc. cit.

16   The chief dates in Jonathan's career are: 1731, wins scholarship from Reading School to St. John's College, Oxford; 1735, B.A., having transferred to Christ Church; 1738, M.A. and Holy Orders; 1743, marries the niece of the Earl of Peterborough, to whose family he had been tutor, receives two livings in Hampshire and becomes Prebendary of Winchester; 1748, D.D. and a Canon of Christ Church; 1760, Dean of Winchester; 1769, Bishop of Llandaff, being translated to St. Asaph later in the same year; 1788, dies at Chilbolton and is buried at Twyford. His apprenticeship as a Stationer is not mentioned in the printed accounts of his life.

17   MS. Trans., 1782–3 (Polite Arts), p. 8.

18   See his letters to Henry Baker, 1747–53, printed *pp. 169–84*.

[ii] *Artistic training and the first London period*

1 Quoted by W. T. Whitley in his typescript notes preserved in the Print Room, British Museum.

2 E. Edwards, *Anecdotes of Painters* (London, 1808), p. xv. This work was completed some years before its publication.

3 W. T. Whitley, *Artists and their Friends in England, 1700–1799* (London 1928), Vol. I, pp. 108–9; E. Waterhouse, *Painting in Britain, 1530–1790* (London 1953), p. 143.

4 R. Dossie, *Memoirs of Agriculture and other Economical Arts*, Vol. III (London, 1782), p. 394; T. Mortimer, *The Universal Director, or the Nobleman and Gentleman's True Guide to the Masters and Professors of the Liberal and Polite Arts and Sciences* . . . (London, 1763), p. 25.

5 E. Edwards, loc. cit. See *pp. 3–4.*

6 M. H. Grant, *Chronological History of the Old English Landscape Painters*, Vol. II, 2nd ed. (Leigh-on-Sea, 1958), p. 117.

7 E. Edwards, op. cit., p. 89; for Redgrave's confusion see ONE: (a) Ref. 8.

8 See W. T. Whitley, op. cit., pp. 15, 17–18, 27.

9 There are no complete lists available of the members of the St. Martin's Lane Academy, but Shipley's name is not given by Vertue (*Walpole Society*, Vol. XXX, Oxford, 1955, p. 171) nor by W. H. Pyne (*Wine and Walnuts*, Vol. II, London, 1824, p. 175). Pyne, however, mentions that Shipley 'studied as a portrait painter under a Mr. Phillips' (ibid., p. 160).

10 Trueman Wood, p. 8.

11 *European Magazine*, 1803, pp. 176–8; partly quoted W. T. Whitley, op. cit., Vol. II, pp. 248–9.

12 There are articles on both the Mosers in the *D.N.B.*

G. M. Moser was to be active in the affairs of the
Society of Arts (see Trueman Wood, pp. 41, 192). For
Old Slaughter's see B. Lillywhite, *London Coffee Houses*
(London, 1963), p. 422.

13 Westminster Public Libraries, Archives Department,
MS. Rate Books of the Parish of St. Anne, Westminster.

14 The Rev. Walter Mildmay was Vicar of Twyford until
his death in 1743. He witnessed Shipley's grandfather's
will in 1726 (see *pp. 22–3* and family tree), and his
nephew, Humphrey Mildmay (d. 1761) owned
Shawford House at Twyford (see *Genealogical
Memoranda relating to the Mildmay Family*, privately
printed, London, 1872).

15 See *pp. 23–4.*

16 Prince Henry Benedict Stuart, Cardinal of York, and
afterwards titular King.

17 See TWO: (i) Ref. 16.

18 *European Magazine*, 1803, loc. cit. Joseph Moser wrote
of this anecdote as being 'a story [that] was once in
circulation'. He could not have participated directly in
the event as he was not born until 1748. He probably
heard about it from his uncle George Michael Moser,
1704–83 (ibid., pp. 83–4).

19 Henry Baker, F.R.S., F.S.A. (1698–1774). See *D.N.B.*

[iii] *The move to Northampton, 1747*

1 S. Whatley, *England's Gazeteer* (London, 1751), Vol. II,
article on Northampton.

2 Thomas Mortimer, *A Concise Account of the Rise, Progress
and Present State of the Society for the Encouragement of Arts,
Manufactures and Commerce* (London, 1763), pp. 2–3.

3 Apart from Vertue's note quoted *p. 25* the only
evidence for Shipley's work as an artist in
Northampton is the farewell notice he inserted in the

Northampton Mercury on 27th May 1754: 'WILLIAM
SHIPLEY, Painter, Lately resident at Northampton,
BEING obliged to settle in London, takes this
Opportunity to thank the Nobility, Gentry, and Others,
who have favoured him with their Commands . . .'.
(Reference supplied through the courtesy of Mr. D.
Howard Halliday, Borough Librarian of Northampton;
this appears to be the only advertisement inserted by
Shipley in the *Mercury*, 1747–54.)

4　See ONE: (a) Ref. 5.

5　See *pp. 169–70*.

6　*Gentleman's Magazine*, Vol. XVI (1746), p. 475.

7　See *pp. 171–2*.

8　Doddridge to Baker, 3rd November 1747 (Ryl. Eng.
MSS. 19; III, 169).

9　Baker to Doddridge, 24th November 1747 (ibid., 179).

10　Doddridge to Baker, 29th January 1747/8 and 11th May
1748 (ibid., 237, 279).

11　For David Erskine Baker (1730–67) see *D.N.B.*

12　H. McLachlan, *English Education under the Test Acts*
(Manchester, 1931), p. 143.

13　T. Mortimer, op. cit., pp. 4, 5.

[*iv*] *Scientific curiosity, 1748–50*

1　See *pp. 169–70*.

2　See *pp. 173–5*.

3　See *pp. 169–70*.

4　Possibly during his visit to London referred to in
Doddridge's Letter to Baker of 11th May 1748 (see
TWO: (iii) Ref. 10).

5　Baker to Doddridge, 6th October 1750 (Ryl. Eng. MSS.
19, IV, 395).

6　Same to same, 24th January 1748/9 (ibid., IV, 4).

7　In his communication to the Royal Society, 16th January

1744/5, 'Of the Wheeler or Wheel Animal'. Printed in his *Employment for the Microscope* (London, 1753), pp. 266–94.

8   Doddridge to Baker, 30th January 1748/9 (Ryl. Eng. MSS. 19, IV, 62).

9   *Gentleman's Magazine*, Vol. XX (1750), p. 89.

10   Baker to Doddridge, 13th February 1749/50 (Ryl. Eng. MSS. 19, IV, 171).

11   William Wilmer of Sywell, Northampton, M.P. for Huntingdon Town from 1734 until his death in 1744.

12   John Conant, 1608–94, Vicar of All Saints, Northampton, from 1671. See *D.N.B.*

13   Doddridge to Baker, 26th March 1750 (Ryl. Eng. MSS. 19, IV, 261).

14   *Gentleman's Magazine*, Vol. XX, p. 137.

15   Doddridge to Baker, 26th March 1750 (Ryl. Eng. MSS., loc. cit.).

16   *Gentleman's Magazine*, Vol. XX, p. 473.

17   Baker to Doddridge, 6th October 1750 (Ryl. Eng. MSS. 19, IV, 395).

18   Doddridge to Baker, 17th October 1750 (Ryl. Eng. MSS. 19, IV, 308; printed *Phil. Trans.*, Vol. XLVI, 1752, pp. 712–21).

19   See the letter from Shipley to Baker, 8th July 1751 (Ryl. Eng. MSS. 19, IV, 339), printed *pp. 179–80*.

20   See *pp. 174–5*.

21   See *pp. 179–80*.

CHAPTER THREE

[v] *The Northampton Fuel Scheme and the 'Proposals', 1751–2*

1   See *pp. 178–9*.

2   Thomas Mortimer, *A Concise Account* [etc.], p. 7.

3   See *pp. 179–80*.

4 'Sea-coal is distinguished from pit-coal, the former . . .
being the product of the Northumbrian pits, the latter
probably coming from the South Staffordshire pits. . . .
It is curious that while sea-coal is always measured by
the Chaldron [36 bushels], pit-coal is weighed by the
ton, the hundred-weight or the load.' J. E. T. Rogers,
A History of Agriculture and Prices, Vol. VII, Part I
(Oxford, 1902), p. 322.

5 T. Mortimer, op. cit., pp. 5–6.

6 J. U. Nef, *The Rise of the British Coal Industry* (London,
1932), Vol. II, p. 260.

7 J. Tucker, 'Instructions for Travellers, 1757', printed in
R. L. Schuyler; *Josiah Tucker, A Selection from His
Economic and Political Writings* (New York, 1931), p. 251.

8 A. Smith, *An Inquiry into the Nature and Causes of the
Wealth of Nations* (Bohn's Standard Library, 1921),
Vol. II, p. 39.

9 Ibid., p. 26; Schuyler, op. cit., pp. 132–3. Tucker was to
become an enthusiastic member of Shipley's Society of
Arts in 1755. Smith was to be concerned with the
foundation of the Edinburgh Society of Arts in the
same year.

10 Mortimer, op. cit., pp. 9–12. The text Mortimer took is
from the pamphlet published in Northampton, 8th June
1753. He says Shipley 'revised' his 'Proposals' before
having them printed.

[vi] *The 'Scheme for putting the Proposals in Execution', 1753*

1 The title which was chosen added 'Commerce' and
omitted 'Sciences', although 'Society of Arts and
Sciences' gained unofficial usage (see Trueman Wood,
p. 18).

2 This idea of 'weighting' the votes of members in
proportion to their subscription was not adopted by the

Society of Arts, which was otherwise modelled on these 'Proposals'.

3 Printed by Thomas Mortimer, *A Concise Account* [etc.], pp. 13–18.

4 See letter from Shipley to Baker, 8th July 1751, printed *pp. 179–80*.

5 Baker's subsequent testimony, printed in J. Nichols, *Literary Anecdotes of the Eighteenth Century*, Vol. V (London, 1812), p. 275.

6 D. G. C. Allan, 'Dr. Hales and the Society, 1753–61; (i) Before the Foundation', *Jnl. R.S.A.*, Vol. CX (1962), p. 857. This article was written before the author had obtained access to the Baker Correspondence in the John Rylands Library, and was uncertain of the identity of the person who gave Shipley his introduction to Hales. For Hales in general see A. E. Clark-Kennedy, *Stephen Hales, D.D., F.R.S.* (Cambridge, 1929).

7 H. F. Berry, *A History of the Royal Dublin Society* (London, 1915), p. 55.

8 S. Madden, *Letter to the Dublin Society on the Improvement of their Fund* (Dublin, 1739), pp. 48–9.

9 Not done by the Dublin Society until the 1760s. See Berry, op. cit., p. 144.

10 The Dublin Society had carried out trials on a machine for measuring the true run of a ship at sea, 1746–60; and in the 1760s it offered premiums for architectural drawings. See Berry, op. cit., pp. 49, 416.

11 See *pp. 179–80*.

12 Mortimer, op. cit., p. 7.

13 Ibid., p. 8.

14 D. G. C. Allan, op. cit. For Yeoman see also E. Robinson, 'The Profession of Civil Engineer in the Eighteenth Century: a Portrait of Thomas Yeoman,

F.R.S., 1704 (?)–1781', *Annals of Science*, Vol. XVIII
(4), 1962.

15 See *pp. 180–4*.

16 Mortimer, op. cit., p. 18.

[*vii*] *The Return to London and the Foundation of the Society of Arts,*
1753–5

1 See notice in *Northampton Mercury*, 24th May 1754,
quoted TWO: (iii), Ref. 3, and the Society's notice *To the*
Publick (*pp. 190–1*), 1754. For details of Great Pulteney
Street see London County Council, *Survey of London*,
Vol. XXXI (1963), p. 126. The Rate Books show that
Messiter had been a householder there since 1749 and
suggest that he lived in what is now No. 13 (Westminster
Public Libraries, Archives Department, MS. Rate Books
of the Parish of St. James, Westminster).

2 Such as Dr. James Parsons in Red Lion Square
(see *pp. 38, 176*).

3 Thomas Mortimer, *A Concise Account* [etc.], p. 8. For
Crisp see A. Cox Johnson, 'The Society and John
Bacon, R.A.', Vol. CX (1962), *Jnl. R.S.A.*, p. 206.

4 A. E. Clark-Kennedy, *Stephen Hales*, p. 223. For the
various London districts of the time see H. Phillips,
Mid-Georgian London (London, 1964).

5 T. Mortimer, loc. cit.

6 London County Council, *Survey of London*, Vol. XXXII
(1963), p. 566.

7 T. Mortimer, op. cit., pp. 18–21.

8 At No. 9. See L.C.C., *Survey of London*, Vol. XXXII,
p. 477.

9 The fourth Parliament of George II was dissolved on
8th April 1754.

10 Johnson's phrase in his celebrated letter on patronage to
Lord Chesterfield, 7th February 1755.

Richard Cosway's portrait of Shipley, painted *c.* 1759–60 and now hanging in the Council Chamber of the Royal Society of Arts.

Detail from James Barry's painting *The Society* (1778) showing Shipley holding *The Instrument of the Institution.*

Textile design by Willi⬚
Pars (premium drawin⬚
for boys under 17, 175⬚

Textile design by J. A.
Gresse (premium draw⬚
for boys under 17, 175⬚

11   T. Stedman, *Letters to and from the Rev. Philip Doddridge, D.D.* (Shrewsbury, 1790), pp. 452–3.

12   R.S.A., Dr. Templeman's Transactions, Vol. I, p. 166. This is the opening of the MS. 'Historical Register' of the Society which supplements Mortimer, p. 21.

13   T. Mortimer, op. cit., p. 22.

14   See *pp. 72–3.*

15   D. G. C. Allan, op. cit., p. 858.

16   Hudson and Luckhurst, p. 7.

17   Soc. Min. (Rough Book). Contrary to Baker's claim of 3rd September 1755, that 'he all along took the minutes' (see J. Nichols, *Literary Anecdotes of the Eighteenth Century*, Vol. V., London, 1812, p. 275 n.), the Rough Minute Book shows that Baker did not take the minutes regularly until 19th February 1755, though he may well have advised Shipley on their wording.

18   It was described as a 'Float . . . to preserve the lives of them that Fall overboard at Sea'. Inquiries 'of Persons skilled in Sea Affairs' were ordered, and a report was to be made at a 'General Meeting' of the Society. Nothing more, however, appears in the Minutes, though, as Trueman Wood suggests (p. 298), this may be the invention for which Shipley received a Silver Medal in 1776.

19   James Theobald (d. 1759) was an active antiquarian. His friendship with Henry Baker is illustrated in correspondence in Ryl. Eng. MSS. 19. Sir Charles Whitworth's association with the Society of Arts is considered in FOUR: (viii).

20   Mortimer, op. cit., pp. 31–2.

CHAPTER FOUR

[viii] Correspondence with Charles Whitworth, 1755

1   For example, in replying to a letter from Charles Powell
    (see below) Shipley was desired by the Society, at a
    meeting on 17th July 1754, to mention its 'infant state'
    (Soc. Min., Rough Book). This was similar to the phrase
    'our infant strength', which he used in his letter inviting
    Benjamin Franklin to become a Corresponding Member.
    See *pp. 195–6*. When Franklin accepted the invitation,
    the Society authorised Henry Baker to draft the reply
    which Shipley was to send (Soc. Min., 18th August 1756).
2   See letters to Shipley from the Bishop of Worcester,
    18th July 1755; Lord Romney, 26th August 1755; and
    Lord Folkestone, 11th October 1753 (G.B. I, 32, 47, 59).
3   Charles Whitworth (*c.* 1721–78) sat in Parliament from
    1747 till 1778, knighted 1768, wrote on commercial and
    parliamentary matters. See *D.N.B.* He was in general a
    supporter of the administration, being distantly connected
    to the Duke of Newcastle's family, and was the receiver
    of a secret service pension. Sir Lewis Namier considered
    him amongst the 'Parliamentary Beggars' in *The Structure
    of Politics at the Accession of George III* (2nd ed., London,
    1957, pp. 418–25).
4   The meeting was concerned with the production of Buff
    leather.
5   Alexander Garden (*c.* 1730–91), physician and botanist.
    See *D.N.B.*
6   Whitworth replied expressing his thanks on 1st July
    (G.B. I, 31).
7   On 25th March 1755, Garden said in a letter to John
    Ellis, 'I wrote Mr. Shipley last year'. (Original at
    Linnean Society, printed Sir J. E. Smith, *A Selection of
    the Correspondence of Linnaeus and other Naturalists,*

London, 1821, Vol. I, p. 342 et seq.) This letter is not amongst the Garden/Shipley letters at the R.S.A.

8   G.B. III, 19.

9   L.A. (M), A1/27.

10   G.B. I, 35.

11   Josiah Tucker (1712–44), economist and divine. See *D.N.B.*

12   Charles Powell (1712–96), of Castell Madoc, see *Dictionary of Welsh Biography*.

13   See M. Edmunds, 'History of the Brecknockshire Agricultural Society, 1755–1955', *Drycheiniog*, Vol. II (1956), pp. 32–7.

14   G.B. I, 42.

15   Ibid., I, 43.

16   Ibid., III, 20.

17   Ibid., I, 44.

18   Soc. Min.

19   Alured Clarke, D.D. (1696–1742). Established a county hospital at Winchester in 1736 and published an account of its management upon which later county hospitals were based. See *D.N.B.*

20   The Society of Arts was often called the 'Premium Society' at this date.

21   G.B. III, 22.

22   Ibid., I, 49.

23   Ibid., I, 50.

24   L.A. (M), A1/33; 6th September 1755.

25   G.B. I, 51; III, 24; I, 53.

26   Soc. Min., 15th October 1755; *Gentleman's Magazine*, Vol. XXV (1755), pp. 505–6.

27   See *pp. 209–10*.

[*ix*] *Secretary and Register, 1755–60*

1   Trueman Wood, pp. 21, 26–7.

2   See *pp. 199–200*.

3   Trueman Wood, p. 22; Hudson and Luckhurst, p. 32.

4   *Rules and Orders of the Society . . . of Arts* [etc.] (London, 1760), pp. 7–11.

5   There follow instructions for the preparation of 'an annual historical Register of the Transactions of the Society' which did not apply in Shipley's years of office.

6   Details follow of the salaries to be paid to the various officers.

7   The various record books which the Assistant Secretary is to keep are listed.

8   How the Collector is to keep and account for these funds is then stated.

9   For quotations unsupported by reference numbers see Soc. Min. under the stated dates.

10 Shipley shared premises with the Society in Craig's Court, Charing Cross, 1755–6, and Castle Court, Strand, 1756–9. See D. G. C. Allan, *The Houses of the Royal Society of Arts* (London, 1966), pp. 4–6.

11 Soc. Min., 2nd March 1757.

12 Ibid., 25th May 1757.

13 To £100 p.a. See Soc. Min., 1st March 1758.

14 Ibid., 1st June 1757. See D. G. C. Allan, 'Dr. Hales and the Society, 1753–61: (ii) After the Foundation', *Journal R.S.A.*, Vol. CXI (1963), p. 55.

15 Soc. Min., 16th, 23rd, 30th November 1757; 4th October, 1st November 1758.

16 Ibid., 20th June, 7th November 1759; 16th June 1760.

17 K. W. Luckhurst, *The Story of Exhibitions* (London, 1951), p. 27.

18 Min. Com. ('Affair of the Porter'), 10th May 1760.

19 In his own right as a member he proposed thirty-two new subscribers between 1754 and 1761.

20 Soc. Min., 15th November 1758.

21 Ibid., 5th January, 1758.

22 Ibid., 20th June and 18th July 1759.

23 For William Davies see *pp. 22–3* and for Charles Lawrence see *pp. 54–5*.

24 Soc. Min., 2nd January and 6th February 1760.

25 Trueman Wood, p. 25.

26 See printed membership *Lists of the Society* [etc.], 8th March 1758 and 5th June 1760.

27 *Rules and Orders of the Society . . . of Arts* [etc.] (London, 1760), p. 6.

28 Soc. Min., 29th November 1758.

29 See *pp. 199–200*.

[x] *'Shipley's School', 1753–8*

1 Even a member, John Ellis, complained in 1759 that 'Our Society has of late become a mere society of drawing, painting and sculpture, and attends to little else, as you may observe by a list of the premiums for this year which I shall send you' (see letter from Ellis to Alexander Garden, 25th August 1759; printed Sir J. E. Smith, *A Selection of Correspondence of Linnaeus and Other Naturalists*, London, 1821, Vol. I, p. 459).

2 See THREE: (vii) Ref. 1.

3 Reference supplied through the courtesy of Mr. D. Howard Halliday, Borough Librarian of Northampton (see *pp. 4, 32*).

4 R. Dossie, *Memoirs of Agriculture and other Economical Arts*, Vol. III (London, 1782), p. 394.

5 Soc. Min., 27th November and 18th December 1754.

6 Trueman Wood, p. 16 and note; G. C. Williamson, *Richard Cosway, R.A.* (London, 1905), pp. 4, 7. See also *p. 85*.

7 Dossie, op. cit., p. 396.

8 William Bailey, *The Advancement of Arts* (London, 1772), p. 338.

9 Soc. Min., 5th March, 16th July, 17th December 1755, 14th January 1756.

10 A list of Shipley's pupils and of the prizes they received from the Society is printed on *pp. 211–18*.

11 Alexander Garden to Shipley, 1st May 1757 (G.B. III, 86).

12 L.A., A1/5. J. Fielding, 1756; for the Universal Register Office see R. L. Melville, *The Life and Work of Sir John Fielding* (London, 1934), pp. 8–26.

13 See *pp. 69–71*.

14 *Public Advertiser*, 25th June, 8th July 1757. Quoted W. T. Whitley, *Artists and Their Friends in England, 1700–1799* (London, 1928), Vol. II, p. 249.

15 William Bailey, the organ-builder, was a member of the Society and a fellow-tenant at the Universal Register Office (see MS. Sub. Bks. and L.A., A1/21. J. Fielding, 1756).

16 *Gentleman's Magazine*, Vol. XXVI (1756), p. 61; R.S.A., Dr. Templeman's Transactions (MS.), I, p. 75. Although this was the official policy of the Society in 1756, it was modified during the subsequent decade to permit the direct encouragement of artistic professions (see Trueman Wood, p. 153).

17 G. C. Williamson, *Life and Works of Ozias Humphry, R.A.* (London, 1918), p. 12. Dr. Williamson made full use of the Humphry MSS. in the Royal Academy Library, and these will be cited hereafter.

18 Humphry MSS., I, 56. Access to these sources was arranged through the courtesy of Mr. S. Hutchison, Librarian to the Royal Academy.

19 Ibid., I, 56. Note on back of letter by Mrs. Humphry.

20   Ibid., I, 59. Ozias Humphry to his parents, 4th October
      1757.
21   Ibid., I, 58. Same to same, 20th September 1757.
22   Ibid., I, 60. Same to same, 29th October 1757.
23   Ibid., I, 64. Mrs. Humphry to Ozias, 15th February 1758.
24   See *Gentleman's Magazine*, Vol. XXVIII (1758), p. 141, and
      Edward Edwards, *Anecdotes of Painters* (London, 1808),
      pp. xvi–xix.
25   R.A., Humphry MSS., I, 65. Shipley to Ozias,
      5th December 1758. William Burgess and William Pars
      will figure in the succeeding part of this chapter.
26   Soc. Min., 9th November 1757; 5th April 1758.

[*xi*] *'Shipley's School', 1758–68*

 1   J. T. Smith, *Nollekens and His Times* (London, 1828),
      Vol. I, p. 3; Vol. II, p. 392.
 2   T. J. Mulvany, *Life of Gandon* (Dublin, 1846), pp. 12,
      213.
 3   The building was subject to so many alterations at this
      time that it would have made a most inconvenient
      headquarters for a large drawing school. Even the
      residential accommodation was scanty (see Soc. Min.,
      7th November 1759).
 4   R. Ackermann, *Repository of Arts*, Vol. I (London, 1809),
      p. 53. John Clarke had paid rates for the premises since
      the early 1750s (Westminster Public Libraries, Archives
      Department, MS. Rate Books of the Parish of St.
      Clement Danes).
 5   Soc. Min., 1st November 1758. See *pp. 71, 82*.
 6   See *pp. 199–200*.
 7   'Mr. Shipley desired to purchase of the Society . . .
      Three Tables with Tressels, Six Benches and a German
      Stove and Mr. Shipley having offered . . . £2 18*s*. . . .
      [Resolved] it will be an advantage to the Society to part

with these things, and that Mr. Shipley had offered their full value' (Soc. Min., 31st December 1760).

8 E. Edwards, *Anecdotes of Painters* (London, 1808), p. xv.

9 T. Jones, 'Memoirs', *Walpole Society*, Vol. XXXII (London, 1951), pp. 7–8.

10 Edwards, op. cit., p. 91.

11 Edwards (loc. cit.) lamented its closing. Dossie refers to several of its pupils as winners of the Society's premiums (*Memoirs of Agriculture*, Vol. III, 1782, p. 391.) But W. H. Pine complained that 'copying plaster casts from the antique was the limit of the practice at Pars's school' (quoted J. L. Roget, *A History of the Old Water-colour Society*, London, Vol. I, p. 138).

12 *Public Advertiser*, 20th May 1762. Quoted by W. T. Whitley in his typescript notes preserved in the Print Room, British Museum.

13 Jones, loc. cit. Jones tells how Charles Powell (see above, *pp. 61–7*) put him in touch with Shipley.

14 Thomas Burgess to the 'Lords and Gentlemen' of the Society, 28th April 1762. L.A., B2/185.

15 Thomas Mortimer, *The Universal Director* [etc.], p. 25; Society of Arts printed membership lists, 1765–7. Lyons Inn was between Holywell Street and Wych Street.

[*xii*] *Relations with the Society of Arts, 1760–78*

1 See *p. 220*.

2 Joseph Moser, character sketch of William Shipley, *European Magazine*, Vol. XLIV (1803), p. 176.

3 Made in his letter of resignation from the office of Register (see *pp. 199–200*).

4 Min. Com. (P.A.), 21st May 1762. Essex House was the surviving portion of the great Thames-side mansion which had been partly demolished in 1682.

5 Soc. Min., 14th June 1762.

6 See FOUR: (xi) Ref. 9.

7 E. Lipson, *The Economic History of England*, Vol. III (London, 1943), p. 151.

8 See *D.N.B.*, and A. H. Samuel, *The Herring* (London, 1918), p. 132.

9 R. Dossie, *Memoirs of Agriculture*, Vol. I, pp. 304–6.

10 Ibid., p. 307. Soc. Min., 15th December 1762.

11 Min. Com. (Misc.), 21st December 1762; 1st February 1763.

12 R. Dossie, op. cit., p. 307.

13 Min. Com. (Misc.), 1st February 1763.

14 Soc. Min., 18th November 1778.

15 MS. Trans. 1776–7, No. 76.

16 See THREE: (vii) Ref. 18.

17 The original MSS. are in MS. Trans., loc. cit., and are printed in *Transactions*, Vol. III (1785), pp. 150–2; the text given here follows the printed version. The 'Account' was reprinted, with an illustration of the model, in *Transactions*, Vol. XXV (1807), pp. 94–6. The silver medal is preserved in the Maidstone Museum.

18 Soc. Min., 24th April and 27th November 1776; Min. Com. (Mech.), 2nd May 1776. Trueman Wood (p. 298) believed the invention was neither 'specially valuable or remarkably original', but see W. Burney (ed.), *New Universal Marine Dictionary* (London, 1815), p. 155.

CHAPTER FIVE

[*xiii*] *Marriage and Maidstone, 1767–86*

1 Trueman Wood, p. 11; Hudson and Luckhurst, p. 33.

2 MS. 'Lectures and Notes' by J. H. Allchin. Also see *pp. 13–14.*

3 J. Chapman, ed., *The Register Book of Marriages belonging to the Parish of St. George, Hanover Square: Vol. I, 1725*

to 1787 (London, Harleian Soc., 1886), p. 170; transcript of the full entry provided by courtesy of Mr. D. Stafford, Vestry Clerk of St. George's.

4   On 16th April 1766 (see MS. Subscription Books).

5   See *pp. 22–3*.

6   M.M., Will of William Shipley, 1802, endorsed 'about £8,000'. In 1788 he inherited £500 from his brother the Bishop of St. Asaph, but this still leaves a considerable sum to be accounted for.

7   Twyford Moors collection: Will of William Davies, 1765. 'Also I give to my nephew William Shipley the sum of £1,000 3% Bank annuities.'

8   See *pp. 51–5*.

9   *England's Gazetteer* (London, 1751), Vol. II, entry under 'Maidstone'.

10 M.M., Rate Books.

11 All Saints' Church, Maidstone, MS. baptismal register and inscriptions on tomb of William Shipley.

12 *Gentleman's Magazine*, Vol. LV (1785), p. 921; Vol. LXV (1795), p. 791.

13 Edward Peale was in partnership from 1795 with P. W. Crowther, Secondary of the Poultry Compter, and John Peale succeeded as Secondary in 1803 (information supplied through courtesy of the Guildhall Library, London). Richard Peale died *c*. 1800 of a cold caught while attending a patient (J. H. Allchin, op. cit., see Ref. 2 above).

14 *Jnl. R.S.A.*, Vol. LXXIII (1925), p. 27.

15 M.M.; J. H. Allchin, op. cit., see Ref. 2 above; Hudson and Luckhurst, p. 33 note.

16 M.M., Rate Books; Brenchley Rent Book.

17 The author's thanks are due to the Company for permitting him to see over Knightrider House in 1965.

18 M.M., Shipley's MS. Memo. Book.

19 Shipley to Samuel More, 22nd December 1778 (MS. Trans., 1779/80, no. 27).

20 See *pp. 201–2.*

21 J. M. Russell, *The History of Maidstone* (Maidstone, 1881), p. 39; *The Topography of Maidstone* (1839), p. 41, says 'the Society commenced about 1783'.

22 They were Valentine Green, F.S.A., Alexander Johnson, LL.D. and M.D., and W. P. Perrin, F.R.S., F.S.A. Lord Romney's second son, the Hon. and Rev. Jacob Marsham, was also a subscribing member of the Maidstone Society. See *pp. 226–7.*

23 Shipley to the Society of Arts, 6th March 1786 (MS. Trans., 1785/6).

24 See *pp. 201–3,* and *Transactions of the Kentish Society* (Maidstone, 1793), p. 4; Thomas Day, *Some Considerations on the different ways of removing Confined and Infectious Air* (Maidstone, 1784), pp. 38, 49–50.

25 Shipley to Arthur Young, 18th May 1785 (B.M., Add. MS. 35, 126 f. 293).

26 See *pp. 113–14.*

27 *Transactions of the Kentish Society,* loc. cit.; M.M., Clement Taylor Smythe MSS., Vol. IV, p. 362; J. M. Russell, op. cit., p. 285.

[*xiv*] *More inventions, 1778–87*

1 Shipley to More, 9th November 1778 (MS. Trans. 1779/80, No. 27).

2 Same to the Society, 2nd December 1778 (MS. Trans., loc. cit.).

3 Including 204 competitors for prizes offered by the Society of Arts in 1874 'for the economical use of fuel in private dwellings' (see Trueman Wood, pp. 489–91).

4 French and Spanish privateers 'infested the sea lanes

around Britain' (see T. S. Ashton, *Economic History of England, the 18th Century*, London, 1955, p. 72).

5 Min. Com. (Mech.), 2nd December 1778.

6 Shipley to More, 16th December, 1778 (MS. Trans., loc. cit.).

7 Shipley wrote what looks like 'Marben', but he probably meant 'Marden', which was a Forest of Dean term for a soft carbonaceous shale (see Geological Survey Memoirs, *Geology of the Forest of Dean Coal and Iron Ore Field*, London, 1942, p. 25; reference supplied through the courtesy of Miss P. Briers, Librarian, the National Coal Board).

8 From the Durham coalfields so named.

9 Shipley to More, 22nd December 1778 (MS. Trans., loc. cit.).

10 Same to the Committee, 13th January 1779 (MS. Trans., loc. cit.).

11 Min. Com. (Mech.), 14th January 1779. The fires were lit in the Great Room following an order made at a Society meeting on the previous day (Soc. Min.).

12 Ibid., 13th January 1780.

13 Ibid., 8th March and 26th April 1781. Shipley was also present at the Committee on 1st March and 5th April.

14 Soc. Min., 12th December 1781.

15 Enquiries kindly undertaken by Miss J. M. Swann, Assistant Curator, Northampton Museum and Art Gallery, and Mr. J. H. Thornton, Head of the Shoe Department, Northampton College of Technology.

16 Shipley probably meant his work for the Maidstone Society and such voluntary services as 'setting down and examining the homes of a Number of the Poor at Maidstone' (see letter to Samuel More, 16th December 1778, MS. Trans., loc. cit.), rather than any remunerative undertaking.

17 George Cockings, Register of the Society since May 1779.

18 Joseph Spackman, Pewterer, of Jewry Street, Aldgate (see *Kent's Directory*, London, 1781).

19 Shipley to the Society, 10th December 1781 (MS. Trans., 1781/2, No. 18).

20 Min. Com. (Ag.), 9th December 1782; Min. Com. (Mech.), 19th December 1782.

21 The invention of William Rich of Yalding (see Soc. Min., 15th February 1786).

22 Min. Com. (Mech.), 26th May 1786. At a meeting of the Society on 31st May 1786 he received thanks from the Chair.

23 His description is preserved in MS. Trans. 1785/6.

[xv] Educational Schemes, 1781–7

1 Shipley to the Society, 25th November 1782 (MS. Trans. 1782/3, No. 8). For the eighteenth-century editions of Locke's *Some Thoughts concerning Education* see H. O. Christophersen, *A Bibliographical Introduction to the Study of John Locke* (Oslo, 1930), p. 101; for some diverse contemporary views on the Grand Tour see A. S. Turberville, ed., *Johnson's England* (Oxford, 1933), Vol. I, pp. 156–8; for charity schools see M. G. Jones, *The Charity School Movement* (Cambridge, 1938).

2 Doddridge had set up a charity school for teaching and clothing the children of the poor in 1737 (*D.N.B.*).

3 Royal College of Veterinary Surgeons, MS. Minutes of the Odiham Society of Agriculture and Industry (founded 1783), 2nd December 1785 and 22nd February 1786 (made available through the courtesy of the Librarian, Miss B. Horder). See also A. Young, *Annals of Agriculture*, Vol. V (London, 1786), p. 285.

4 See *pp. 205–6*.

5   Soc. Min., 28th February 1781; Min. Com. (P.A.), 10th March 1781.

6   Edward Hooper, a Vice-President of the Society since 1758, took the Chair on 14th March 1781 (see Soc. Min.).

7   See *pp. 23–4*.

8   Hudson and Luckhurst, p. 365. The membership began to increase again after 1784.

9   Alexander Pope, *Epistles to Several Persons* (Twickenham Edition, 1951), p. 156.

10 Min. Com. (P.A.), 10th December 1782; Soc. Min., 4th, 11th, 18th December 1782.

11 Min. Com. (P.A.), 19th December 1786. Shipley was not present at the judging although he was among a number of members especially invited to attend (ibid., 12th December 1786). The occasion has been referred to in print (see Trueman Wood, p. 312; *Jnl. R.S.A.*, Vol. XC (1942), pp.8, 87), but Shipley's work as the originator has so far remained unrecorded.

12 See Letter from Professor John Symonds to Arthur Young, December 1786, printed M. Betham Edwards, *Autobiography of Arthur Young* (London, 1898), pp. 147–8.

13 Harry Chester's address to the Society, 16th November 1853, *Jnl. S. of A.*, Vol. II (1854), pp. 1–6. Chester was himself unaware of Shipley's educational schemes, and therefore innocent of irony when saying 'we shall not think it necessary to pursue the very objects William Shipley pursued . . . We hope however to do some things that Shipley and his coadjutors would have gladly seen done'.

14 Min. Com. (Misc.), 22nd August 1787.

[*xvi*] *The Closing Years, 1788–1803*

1   J. M. Russell, *The History of Maidstone*, p. 392;

Transactions of the Kentish Society (Maidstone, 1793), p. 5; M.M., Collection of printed notices issued by the Maidstone and Kentish Societies.

2 B.M., Add. MS. 33, 978, f. 178. The letter informed Banks that on the recommendation of Dr. S. F. Simmons, F.R.S., he had been unanimously elected an honorary member of the Kentish Society. It was written by a scribe but is signed with Shipley's name and designation 'Treasurer to the Society'.

3 Jones to Shipley, 27th September 1788, printed in Teignmouth, *Memoirs of the Life, Writings and Correspondence of Sir William Jones* (London, 1806), Vol. II, p. 167. Jones had been exchanging letters with Shipley since 1786 (see ibid., p. 103, when he apologises for his delay in answering 'your excellent letters from Maidstone'; reference supplied through the courtesy of Prof. Garland Cannon, Queens College, City University of New York). He was a corresponding member of the Kentish Society. See *p. 102*.

4 M.M., op. cit.

5 See articles on Jonathan Shipley and William Davies Shipley in *D.N.B.*

6 See G. Cannon, *Oriental Jones* (London, 1964), pp. 82, 108.

7 Shipley sent him accounts of useful inventions which he hoped would be of value in India (see Lord Teignmouth, loc. cit.). Jones founded the 'Society for enquiring into the History, Civil and Natural, the Antiquities, Arts, Sciences, and Literature of Asia' in 1784 (see Cannon, op. cit., p. 114).

8 Franklin corresponded with Shipley over his membership of the Society of Arts in 1755 (see *pp. 195-8* and L. W. Labaree, ed., *The Papers of Benjamin Franklin*, Vol. VI (New Haven, 1963), pp. 186-9, 499-500) and in 1786 he

became a member of the Maidstone Society. Franklin's plans for colonial reform were mentioned by Shipley to Dr. Samuel Madden in 1757. Madden commented: 'I am rejoiced at Mr. Franklin's coming over with so good a Plan which to the shame of Governments has been overlooked such a number of years. If our Colonies be not properly modelled and protected nothing but Ruin and disgrace can follow . . .' (Madden to Shipley 26th November 1759, G.B. III, 119).

9　See above, *p. 108*.

10　See FOUR: (viii), Ref. 5.

11　William Hazlitt, 1737–1820, father of the essayist, was at Maidstone from 1770 to 1780 (Margaret Hazlitt's MS. 'Recollections', preserved in the University of Delaware). In 1778 Shipley signed a trust deed on Hazlitt's behalf (M.M., Hazlitt MSS.; reference supplied through the courtesy of Mr. L. R. A. Grove).

12　*European Magazine*, Vol. XLIV (1803), pp. 176–7.

13　Jones to Shipley, 11th October, 1790 (printed Teignmouth, op. cit., p. 202).

14　M.M., Shipley's Memo Book, f. 35. For the French original see R. Caillois, *Œuvres Complètes de Montesquieu*, Vol. I, p. 295.

15　On 6th December; for details of the Bishop's family see N. Tucker's valuable article in *Jnl. Flintshire Hist. Soc.*, Vol. XX (1962), pp. 9–26.

16　L.A., Red Book, No. 27.

17　Shipley to Thomas Marsham, Secretary of the Linnean Society, 9th May 1796 (Linnean Society Archives, made available through the courtesy of the General Secretary, Mr. T. O'Grady); Shipley had been elected F.L.S. on 16th October 1792, but did not keep up his subscription payments. He sent two guineas 'in composition with his letter of resignation'.

Landscape with cottage, surrounded by trees by Barbara Marsden
(premium drawing for girls under 14, 1755).

Composition after Nature of Beasts and Birds by Nathaniel Smith
(premium drawing for youths under 21, 1759).

Ozias Humphry. Engraving by D. P. Pariset from P. E. Falconet's drawing of 1768.

Faun with kid by Joseph Nollekens (premium drawing for youths under 22, 1759).

18 'Either from want of a full attendance, or of subscriptions, their efforts were not attended with the desired success', J. Boys, *General View of the Agriculture of the County of Kent* (London, 1796), p. 213. A printed notice issued by the Society which contains Shipley's name as a Committee Member is preserved in the Maidstone Museum.

19 9th January 1794: 'Edwards told me Mr. Shipley, who founded the Drawing School in the Strand, where several artists of reputation received their first instruction, is still living, and is about 84 years of age.' James Greig, ed., *The Farington Diary* (London, 1922), Vol. I, p. 33.

20 T. Jones, 'Memoirs', *Walpole Society*, Vol. XXXII (1951), pp. 7–8.

21 The 'late Keeper of the Royal Academy' was G. M. Moser, uncle to Joseph (see TWO: (ii), where the story of Shipley's arrest is quoted); see *The Spectator*, No. 1, 1st March 1710/11, for *The Spectator*'s taciturnity.

22 Min. Com. (Misc.), 24th February 1803.

23 *Monthly Magazine*, Vol. XV (1803), p. 561.

24 Brief obituary notices referring to his age and his work as Founder of the Society of Arts appeared in the *Kentish Gazette* 3rd January 1804, the *Monthly Magazine*, Vol. XVI (1804), p. 96, the *European Magazine*, Vol. XLV (1804), p. 78, and the *Gentleman's Magazine*, Vol. LXXIV (1804), p. 88, the last mistaking Maidstone for Manchester, an error which was copied in the *Dictionary of Natural Biography*.

DOCUMENTS

1 Constitution and Regulations of the proposed Chamber of Arts, 1722.

2 Philip Peck's Proposal for Encouragement of Arts and Sciences by the Royal Society, 1738.

3 Letters exchanged by Shipley and Henry Baker, 1747–53.

4 Minutes of the First Meeting of the Society of Arts.

5 First Notice published by the Society of Arts.

6 The 'Plan' of the Society of Arts, 1755.

7 Shipley's first letter to Benjamin Franklin.

8 Shipley's Letters of Resignation.

9 Shipley's Plan to extend the Maidstone Society, 1786.

The documents printed below illustrate Shipley's life with particular reference to the foundation and working of the Society of Arts. Most of them come from Shipley's pen and the exceptions (1, 2, and 6) clarify the development of his central idea. The Regulations of the Chamber of Arts (1) and Philip Peck's Proposal (2) give little known details of two important precedents for Shipley's achievement, which is itself illustrated in (3), (4), (5) and (6). The first of these sections is the longest and the least known; it consists of the previously unpublished correspondence between Shipley and Baker, for the crucial years 1747 to 1753, and shows the extent of Shipley's knowledge and interests when he was still at the periphery of organised science in England. The first minutes and first notice (4 and 5) of the Society of Arts have often been partly quoted or paraphrased. Their complete texts are given here, together with Baker's 'Plan' (6), so that the reader may have to hand the working instruments of the Society's early years.

Shipley's letter to Benjamin Franklin (7), though familiar in the context of Franklin's membership of the Society of Arts, deserves reconsideration as an example of Shipley's own exertions as the Society's Secretary. His two letters of resignation from the Society's administration, the second and longer being unprinted till now (8), marked a turning point in the story of his life. The fundamental continuity of his interests and aspirations is shown in the last document (9), his pamphlet proposing the extension of the Maidstone Society which he published in 1786 when he was seventy-one years of age.

[1]

CONSTITUTION AND REGULATIONS OF THE PROPOSED CHAMBER OF ARTS, 1722*

* Reprinted from *Three Letters concerning the Forming of a Society, to be called The Chamber of Arts, for the Preserving and Improvement of Operative Knowledge, the Mechanical Arts, Inventions and Manufacture* (London, 1722), pp. 12–15.

An ESSAY towards a CONSTITUTION for regulating this SOCIETY

The Preamble to the Subscription Book

WHEREAS our famous ROYAL SOCIETY has made the most wonderful Progress in their Inquisition of Causes, and thereby laid open a large Field to Mankind, in order for the Production of Effects, which has not been yet equal to the former, for Want of the United Labours of many, and the Support of a Publick Purse. And

Whereas several ingenious and useful Arts have been lost for Want of due Care in preserving them, many promising Undertakings dropt in *Embrio* for Want of Application and Improvement, and a great Number of envious Artists and Mechanicks have either wasted much Time and Study, (being unacquainted with the Principles of Philosophy) or labour'd under unsurmountable Difficulties in bringing their Projects to Maturity for Want of proper Means to try Experiments.

Therefore, out of a Consideration for the Publick Good, and for the Promoting, Preserving, and Improvement of Operative Knowledge, the Mechanical Arts, Inventions and Manufactures,

We whose Names are hereunto Subscrib'd, do form ourselves into a Society: The Meeting-Place whereof to be call'd *The Chamber of* ARTS: And for these Purposes do Voluntarily agree to Contribute Annually the respective Sums against our Names, over and above what we shall have paid at our Admittance, on Forfeiture of what we shall have before paid and contributed, and of having our Names Eraz'd from this Subscription.

Standing Regulations for the Members of
 The Chamber of Arts

I THAT the Promoting, Preserving, and Improvement, of Operative Knowledge, the Mechanical Arts, Inventions, and Manufactures, shall be the Business of this Society.

II That they take an Account of the present State of the Mechanical Arts, Inventions, and Manufactures, and search after and endeavour to recover those that are lost, and keep Registers with proper Models, Descriptions, and Narratives of the Manner of performing every Thing Useful, Curious, and Rare.

III   That in the Promoting of Operative Knowledge, they have a particular Regard to the Transactions and Judgment of the *Royal-Society*, and make such Experiments as may be recommended by them, and appear of Use to the Designs of this SOCIETY.

IV   That they invite curious Artists and Mechanicks, as well Foreigners as others, to apply to them, and be at the Charge of promoting, encouraging, and making Experiments in any Thing New, Useful, and Curious, that they may have to propose and that shall appear reasonable to the SOCIETY, by Agreement with the *Inventor*.

V   That they keep a Register of all the Experiments they make, as well of those that have not succeeded to the Design propos'd, as of those that have, they often being of universal Consequence, and directing to the Invention of other Experiments.

VI   That those who are admitted Members of this SOCIETY may pay on their Admittance any Sum they think proper, and subscribe to pay each *per Ann*. Half-yearly.

VII   That the SOCIETY meet once every Week at such Time and Place as the Majority shall agree to, but that not less than Five shall sit to do Business.

VIII   That two or more Members of the SOCIETY shall be yearly appointed Treasurers; and that no Money shall be issu'd by the Treasurers but what appears order'd in the Minute-Books of the SOCIETY; and that all Sums of Money belonging to the SOCIETY over and above the Sum of £100 for necessary Expences, shall be lodg'd in the *Bank* in the Names of the Treasurers.

ix   That two Members of the SOCIETY be appointed Secretaries; the one for Domestick Affairs, the other for Foreign Correspondencies: That they attend all Meetings of the SOCIETY or Committees of the same, when order'd so to do; and that the Secretary for Domestick Affairs keep the Registers of the SOCIETY; entering therein only such Things as they shall order; and that he keep the Accompts of the SOCIETY, and have the Care of collecting the Annual Subscriptions, paying the same Weekly into the Hands of the Treasurers; and also that he Summons the Members to all General Meetings when order'd by the SOCIETY, or when any Five Members require the same under their Hands.

x   That a Chair-Man be appointed every Month, and that he take Care all Debates are regular: That a Successor be chose the last Day of his Sitting; and at the same Time, that the Secretary enter a State of the SOCIETY's Cash in the Minute-Book.

xi   That all Questions in Dispute be determin'd by Ballot; and every new Member chosen by Ballot, be first propos'd at two several Meetings.

xii   That no New Agreement be made, or Proposal accepted, unless the same be agreed to at two several Meetings.

xiii   That the SOCIETY engage Correspondents among the Ingenious and Curious in all Countries.

xiv   That they strike a Medal proper to the Designs of the SOCIETY, and distribute one to each Member on his Admission, and to every Person Abroad accepted as a Correspondent.

xv   That any Person applying to the SOCIETY, and producing

any Thing New, Useful, and Curious, and presenting the SOCIETY with a Model, Draught, or proper Explication of the same, shall have the SOCIETY's Medal presented him, and be enter'd as a Donor in the Books of the SOCIETY.

XVI That any Person being the Inventor of any New Tool, or Instrument in Workmanship, or Husbandry, presenting a Model of the same to the SOCIETY, shall have a proper Reward, and be enter'd in the Registers of the SOCIETY as the Inventor of the same.

XVII That any Member of the SOCIETY being the Inventor or Improver of any Thing Useful and Curious, and which can be reduc'd to Practice for the Benefit of the Publick, shall have a Medal struck on that Occasion expressive of the same, and be enter'd in the Books of the SOCIETY as a Benefactor to the Publick.

XVIII That for the regular carrying on the Business of the SOCIETY, the following Committees be standing Committees: That three Persons be especially appointed for each Committee, but that any other Members may attend the same.

A Committee for the Registers.
A Committee for the Improvement of Manufactures.
A Committee for New Experiments and Inventions.
A Committee for Correspondencies.

XIX That when it shall appear necessary to alter or add to these Standing Regulations, such Alteration and Addition shall be propos'd at two General Meetings; and at the Second be determin'd by Ballot.

FINIS

[2]

PHILIP PECK'S PROPOSAL, 1738*

A Proposal for Encouragement of Arts and Sciences by the Royal Society.

That One Thousand pounds be raised by such Members, as please to Advance the same to be Employed to Assist persons producing New and Useful Inventions.

That a Committee be appointed for said purpose to meet weekly or oftener, and when the Inventions proposed to them appears new and Beneficial to the Public, the Inventor to be Assisted with money to procure a Patent reserving a share or Yearly sum out of the produce to be added to the said Capital Fund or Stock of £1,000.

That after all charges are deducted and an allowance made to the Royal Society towards their general charges—the Surplus or profits arising by the said Fund of £1,000 be divided at such times and proportions as shall be agreed, by a Majority of the Proprietors thereof, at a General Meeting to be held for that purpose.

---

* Royal Society, Misc. MSS. Vol. IV, No. 57. (Copyright reserved to the Royal Society.)

[3]

LETTERS EXCHANGED BY SHIPLEY AND HENRY BAKER, 1747–53*

Letter I: Shipley to Baker

Northampton,
October the 18th, 1747

Sir,

Since I have been here, I have, according to promise, enquired after some Fossils. I have procured some Stones from a Quarry near Northampton that contain a variety of Petrified shells and also some Kettering Stone, the same which Dr. Hook describes, which if you have none of it, I believe it deserves a place in your collection.[1]

I believe I shall shortly take a Tour into Staffordshire. I am told that there the Mines abound with Fossils. If so I'll endeavour to procure some from the miners that shall be worth your notice.

As, Sir, you have a taste that is insatiable for all manner of natural curiosities, and have always been ready to communicate your ingenious sentiments to others, I suppose that what I have to mention will not be unacceptable. We have in Northampton a Society of Gentlemen that are very much addicted to all manner of Natural Knowledge. I may call it the Royal Society in miniature, in number about 30. There belongs to it some Gentlemen of the best fortunes of any in Northamptonshire, amongst which are Sir Arthur Harsley, Hanborough, Jeykill, Laughton, and several other Esquires. I think the most curious Gentleman amongst them is Doctor Doddridge a

* Published by kind permission of the John Rylands Library in Manchester, where the originals are preserved.

Dissenting Minister and Master of a very large Academy for the Education of Young Gentlemen.[2]

The Gentlemen of this Society, not content with examining into Nature themselves, are also desirous of having the opinions of the Curious on that subject. They correspond with many eminent Gentlemen in several parts of this Kingdom. Last Tuesday at their weekly meeting some of the Gentlemen, Hearing that I had the Honour of your Acquaintance, asked me if I thought that their correspondence with you would be agreable. I answered I thought it would, and undertook to write to you on that subject for which I received the thanks of the whole Society. If, Sir, you approve of their proposal the Gentlemen will by their President send you an Account of any new discovery they shall make or any uncommon Fossil they shall procure provided they shall have doublets thereof.

I have made a proposal for the having a Prize Medal Annually. They seem much to approve of it and next Tuesday it is to be put to the vote. I shall be glad, Sir, of your answer to this proposal, at any time when you have leisure, which I shall make known to the Gentlemen of the Society. I believe nothing will be so entertaining to them as the sight of some of your Mixtures of Salts.[3] If you approve of sending two or three vials of them a Friend of mine shall call for them who will send them to me with some other things. I believe, Sir, I remember your method with them, oth[herwise] a short direction will enable the President to show them to the Society.

Pray my compliments to Mrs. Baker, Dr. Parsons, Dr. Stuart, etc.[4]

I remain, Sir,
Your most Humble Servant,

W. SHIPLEY

Direct for me at Mr. Quenby's[5] in the Drapery in Northampton. P.S.—Doctor Doddridge seems very desirous of your correspondence.[6]

Letter II: Baker to Shipley (Draft)

London, Oct. 22nd, 1747

Sir,

I had the Favour of yours on Monday, and think myself much obliged to the Gentlemen of the Society you mention for honouring me with an Offer of their Correspondence[1] which I would be greatly neglectful of my own Pleasure and Improvement if I did not willingly embrace.

Nothing can promote knowledge and discover Truth as much as a mutual Communication of Observations made by People in the same Enquiries. Whatever therefore you shall be pleased to send me that is either curious in itself or can aid in any Manner to rectify a Mistake or inform of something not so well known without it, I shall if you give me leave communicate in your name to the Royal Society where I can assure it a candid and kind Reception, and in return I shall willingly transmit to them anything of a like nature as shall be brought by the said Society or come to my knowledge by them. I must only beg that the Gentlemen will indulge me a little as to Regularity of Time and be so good as to accept Accounts of things as I can find opportunity to write. For you, I believe, are sufficiently sensible, my Correspondencies are so many both in England and in foreign parts, I have so much Company, when I am at home and am engaged in so much Business abroad, my Hours are seldom at my own Command which obliges me to trespass on all my friends by turns: though sooner or later they are sure of all the Services in my Power.

I entreat you therefore to apprize the Gentlemen of this lest they should mistake Necessity for Negligence or disrespect. I must desire you likewise to inform them that having been some time preparing for the Press a full Account of my

Experiments on Salts and Saline Bodies, I have never parted with any of the Preparations out of my own Hands even to the Royal Society that was pleased to bestow on me a Gold Medal for the Experiments on those subjects I showed before them. I fear I should anticipate my own work, for which Reason I must hope that your Society will excuse me at present on my Promise that when my Book is finished I will send them a collection of the most remarkable things which I mention therein.[2]

Pray make my best Compliments Acceptable to the whole Society and to every Member thereof and inform them how sensible I am of their great kindness and civility in desiring to supply my little Collection with what things they can spare from theirs, and assure them on my part I will seek out an Occasion of sending them any Curiosity I can meet with, desiring their Acceptance of all I can procure a Duplicate.

And now Sir I have to thank you for what you have already picked up for me and for your promise to remember me in Staffordshire, where there are a variety of figured Fossils, Metals, Minerals. Iron Stones in particular are when broken frequently marked with fair Impressions of Plants. I beg you will inquire after and also for different species of Echinite, Ammonite, Shells, Petrefactions, Tiles, Spars and Chrystals: and whatever expense you will be at in Carriage etc. I will thankfully repay, when I shall have the Pleasure to assure you in London with how much Esteem I am

Dear Sir
Your most humble servant,

[HENRY BAKER]

Any Commands from Dr. Doddridge will be a favour to his humble servant.[3]

Oct. 22nd 1747.

Letter III: Shipley to Baker

Northampton, May the 10th [1748]

Dear Sir,

As you was sometimes since so free as to offer your assistance in anything relating to the Philosophical Society at Northampton, I being now myself a member thereof, make bold to trouble you concerning an improvement I have endeavoured to make on the Barometer. I suppose it may be effected by a fluid floating on the Mercury which by a contrivance in the Tube shall make the Spirit rise and fall so many times more than the Mercury in common Barometers, as the Specific gravity of the Fluid is less than the Mercury. The form of the Barometer is as follows:—

At the Height of about $27\frac{1}{2}''$, somewhat at below where the Mercury subsides when lowest in common Barometers, I propose to have a Cylindrical Box, as at A, which shall be about four times in Diameter larger than the upper Tube, which perhaps will be large enough for the purpose. Upon this box there must be a Tube about three Feet in Length or longer as is required.

I suppose that the atmosphere pressing on the external Mercury in the Bason, B, and elevating the Fluid in the Box, A, if it is 16 times lighter than the Mercury, will be elevated in the Tube, C, 16 times higher from the Box than the Mercury alone would rise by the same Pressure of the Atmosphere.

Please, Sir, at any time when you have leisure to let me hear your sentiments on it, I don't doubt but you'll presently perceive whether it is practicable or not. Please, also, if you think it practicable, when you see Mr. Cuff[1] next to ask him what he thinks will be the Price of a Barometer made after this form. For our Society is desirous to have one if it can be brought to perfection. We have appointed one whose particular Business it is to keep a Journal of the weather, and imagine that a Barometer made after this form may enable Him to make nicer observations on the alterations of the Atmosphere.

Pray my compliments to Dr. Parsons, and the casts of the medals that I promised him shall shortly be sent. Had I not been obliged to go out of town on some extraordinary Business they had certainly been done when I was in London.

When you write, please, Sir, to send me a direction for the Doctor for I have forgot the name of the Square where the Doctor lives.

'I suppose the Cylindrical Box need be no longer than the difference between the Mercury when at Highest & lowest in common Barometers.'

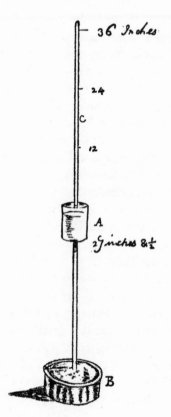

Shipley's barometer; diagram and note accompanying Letter III

When I go into Staffordshire I'll not fail to enquire amongst the miners for the Fossils you mentioned. Esquire Lawton,[2] a very ingenious Gentleman, who resides at present in Northampton and belongs to our Society, is going shortly to live in Derbyshire, I have engaged him to send me for you what Fossils he can collect.

Pray my compliments to Mrs. Baker and all Friends, I remain,

Dear Sir,
Your most Humble Servant to command,
W. SHIPLEY

Direct for me at Mr. Braifields[3] in the Drapery in Northampton.

(Drawing of barometer accompanies this letter)

Letter IV: Baker to Shipley (Draft)

To Mr. Shipley
London, June 28th, 1748

Dear Sir,

My long Delay in answering yours has been wholly owing to a Desire of giving you all the Satisfaction possible in Relation to your new-constructed Barometer which I would not do without consulting Workmen as well as Philosophers, and you know that Tradesmen of all Arts are not over hasty in Matters which require consideration and are out of the common Road. Mr. Cuff[1] and the People he employs were a long time puzzling their Heads about it, and declared at last that such an Instrument would be very troublesome to make, and impossible to be sent into the Country, and that if made it would differ very little in its Effects from the Common Barometer. I was however unwilling to be wholly determined by their Opinion, and therefore consulted my most valuable and ingenious friend Mr. Folkes,[2] who after taking some Days to consider the Matter thoroughly, has set it in a true light by showing from a way of Reasoning, amounting nearly to a Proof, that the lighter fluid will not rise as you imagine in the same Proportion as the respective Gravity of one to the other, but that its rising and falling will be in a compound Ratio of their different Gravities, which will render it so complicated that it will prove extremely difficult if not almost impracticable to form a scale whereby it can be made more desirable than our present Barometers. It may however certainly be made, but then the Tubes must be filled and the Parts put together in the Place where it is to stand, and being a Thing out of the way, it will I doubt be pretty expensive, unless you can perform most of the troublesome Work yourself.

It has given me much uneasiness that I could not write a full Answer sooner. I am also greatly ashamed that I have not yet returned my Acknowledgments to good Dr. Doddridge for his last favour, which I am therefore afraid he must think me highly undeserving. But when you assure him of my utmost Esteem and Respect and let him know that I have not his happy capacity of being able to recollect myself sufficiently after a Variety of Different Avocations which every Day brings along with it, to sit down and express myself as I wish to do when I write to him, I hope he will excuse my Silence. I flattered myself indeed that I might probably have seen him at London before now. I beg you likewise to pay my Compliments to Mr. Lawton and thank him for the Fossils he lately sent me. I had the pleasure of seeing him several Times when he was at London and found him to be a very sensible and ingenious man, and he was so obliging to promise me what Fossils he can collect in Derbyshire, in return of which I should be glad if it were in my Power to do him any kind of Service.

I hope you enjoy your Health and are very happy in the Country. Dr. Parsons lives in Red Lion Square and will be very thankful for the Casts you intend him. I should likewise myself be very glad of any you have to spare which you have not favoured me with already, and in particular the Heads of all the Roman Ladies would be highly acceptable.

I have some slight remembrance of your mentioning to me the Impression of a Fish in Coal and wish you could procure it for me. And if you are able to make me up a little Boxfull of any thing, and will send it by the Carrier, I will pay you with many Thanks whatever Expense you may be at.

And now, Sir, wishing you every good you can wish yourself I will detain you no longer, but to assure you I am with much Regard,

Your most affectionate humble Servant.

Strand, June 28th, 1748

Letter V: Shipley to Baker

Northampton, July 3rd, 1748

Dear Sir,

I received yours and own myself extremely obliged to you for your care in procuring me so accurate an account concerning the Barometer. But at the same time must beg your pardon for offering to your consideration as my original contrivance what Doctor Doddridge now informs me Descartes hath long since published to the world.[1] But I hope, Sir, your candour will excuse it when I mention that after having accidentally thought of it without the least knowledge of Descartes Scheme, I communicated it to Dr. Doddridge, Mr. Lawton and several other of my correspondence, who all thought it might be put in practice and esteemed it a new contrivance. Then Sir, but not till then, I took the freedom to offer it to your consideration.

Last night, as I spent the evening with Doctor Doddridge we drank your health several times. The Doctor intends shortly to set out for London. He proposes to himself the greatest pleasure in meeting 'his most worthy and Ingenious Friend' as he always styles him.[2]

I will not fail to send the Empresses Heads with several other things as soon as I can possibly get them Finished.

I am, with my compliments to Mrs. Baker, etc.

Dear Sir,

Your most Humble Servant,

W. SHIPLEY

Michelangelo's seal: drawing of Pier Maria da Pescia's intaglio (reproduced from Forrer's Biographical Dictionary of Medallists *by courtesy of the Victoria and Albert Museum)*

Letter VI: same to same

Northampton, June 5th, 1751

Dear Sir,

I take the opportunity to write per Dr. Doddridge, and had sent you several impressions of antique Gems, had I not been very much engaged in a variety of Business, but will not fail to send them the first opportunity.

If, Sir, you examine Michelangelo's Seal[1] with a good glass you'll find the Workmanship admirable.

The Gentleman that owns the Egyptian Coin is not willing to part with it. It was ploughed up in a field near Stamford in Lincolnshire, where Roman coins are often found. The reverse was quite plain. It seemed to be pure gold without any alloy, and might be bent as easy as a Ducket.

> I am,
>
> With my Compliments to Mrs. Baker and your Sons,[2]
> Your most Humble Servant,
>
> W. SHIPLEY

Letter VII: same to same

Northampton, July 8th, 1751

Dear Sir,

I have at last finished your Collection of Antique Gems. They had been sent last Wednesday as I proposed, but some of my Dyes broke in making the impressions. I did all that lay in my power to get them ready to send them on Friday last, but the Plaster of Paris was not hard enough for my Purpose.

I hope, Sir, you'll excuse my not sending them by the time proposed, as it was not owing to any neglect but entirely to an accident. There is one Hundred of the best of my collection enclosed in a Cabinet with five Drawers, all stained of a fine red. The Gems being set on a ground of that Colour gives them a very pretty appearance.

In large Sets as yours of the Roman Commonwealth and Empire its impossible but there must be some of inferior workmanship. But as there are so many Capital ones amongst them I believe that you'll think on the whole that yours is a very good Collection. They are most of them made from sulphurs cast by Baron Stosch.[1] What defects you see in any of them were in the Sulphurs, but those that I have cast from the original Gems or Pastes are quite perfect without any defects.

My proposals are much approved by Gentlemen of Fortune and taste. Whenever, Sir, you do me the favour to oblige me with materials from the Dublin Society[2] for a Scheme to put them in execution, I'll immediately follow your advice in applying to Dr. Hales.[3]

I believe if there should not be money enough collected to make this Scheme General, a beginning might very well be made by encouraging some things that shall be thought of the greatest consequence to the Nation. Dr. Hales particularly recommends Naval Improvements I believe. As this is a maritime nation no improvements can be of greater consequence than those of that kind. I shall be much obliged, Sir, if you'll let me know if you receive the Box safe.

Please also let me know if my proposals are approved by the Gentlemen of your acquaintance. The Gems were sent to the Coach last night and directed to you Carriage paid.

I am, with my Humble Service to Mrs. Baker

Sir,

Your most obedient Humble Servant,

W. SHIPLEY

Letter VIII: same to same

Northampton, August 12th, 1753

Dear Sir,

I am just returned from my journey into Hampshire, and have picked up a few Fossils, but I am afraid that they are not worth your acceptance.

I returned through Wiltshire and was highly entertained with several very remarkable Pieces of British Antiquity, some of which I shall briefly describe, which are Stonehenge,

Wansdyke, and some Antiquities at and round about Avebury.[1]

I took particular notice of Stonehenge, to observe if the stones were natural or artificial, and was presently convinced by their Veins, their Beds and their Laminas that they were natural.

Wansdyke is a mighty Trench of about fifty or sixty miles in length and about 25 feet deep. The Parapet is on the South side and about 12 feet high. I believe it was made to check the invasions of the Northern Nations.

At Avebury the Temple of the Sun very much engaged my attention. I had mistook it for a fortification, but I observed that the parapet was on the outward edge of the Ditch, which if so must have given the besiegers much the advantage of the besieged. The parapet is about 20 feet high, and the Ditch about 30 feet deep. The Temple is circular, and about 600 yards in diameter. All round the outward side of the Ditch, viz. from the top of the parapet to the bottom of the Ditch the Sun's rays are curiously cut.

In the Slope not far from the Temple of the Sun is a Royal Barrow 120 feet high. Though it was very steep yet I went to the top of a serpentine walk, where I found an Altar which was an exact Hexagon. On the sides of the Hill were six Buttresses that reached from the Bottom to the top of the Hill, and answered exactly to the six sides of the Altar.

The Stones at Avebury are very numerous, and some of them much larger than any at Stonehenge. The Avebury men told me, that within this two or three years a fellow had taught them the method of breaking them to pieces, which is by making fires round them and striking them with very large sledge Hammers while they are hot; and then by that means break them which would otherwise be impracticable. They have already made terrible havoc with them and built several Houses with the pieces, in a few years I believe they will destroy them all.

For about twelve miles northwards of Avebury on many of the Downs I observed an innumerable number of lesser stones which the Country People call *grey weathers*. Though they are scattered very irregularly, I observed this particular in all the parcels that I met with. The greatest part of them lay very near one to the other, the rest lay thinly scattered, some in small parcels at a considerable distance from the large parcels and others lying singly at a much greater distance. I fancied that these stones might possibly be monuments of the Dead, slain in Battle and that they were erected on the very places where they fell. The large parcel might represent where the main body of the Army engaged, the lesser parcels skirmishes, and the single ones at a distance might be placed in commemoration of those that fell either pursuing or being pursued. I also took notice of their different sizes. There were some few of about five or six tons weight, which I thought might be for Officers of distinction. A considerable number were about 1000 or 1500 weight, these were perhaps for Officers of inferior rank. All the others were I believe on an average one with another about two or three Hundred weight which might be for the common men. What seemed to confirm me in this opinion was this. There were always camps near these parcels of stones but no Barrows, which are almost always found near other Camps.

The Country People all believe that these Stones grew on the Downs. I had a very good opportunity of satisfying myself as to that particular. On one of the Downs some masons were raising some stones with Crow-Bars, and breaking them to pieces for to build with. I viewed the Bottoms of them and observed, so far as they lay under the surface of the ground, that their irregular corners were as sharp as if just taken out of the Quarry, but the corners of the upper surfaces were almost worn smooth with time. I also observed several pieces of the stones which the Masons broke off with their sledge

Hammers, and could plainly observe their veins and Beds that correspond with some kinds of stone that I have seen that were dug out of Quarries. I believe, Sir, that you'll allow that all stones that have any kind of vegetation have coats similar to flints and pebbles and of a different texture from the stone, but these stones are of the very same texture from the middle to the surface.

I have received a letter from Dr. Wall of Worcester,[2] and also two others from Dr. Hales concerning my Proposals. They both give me the greatest encouragement to proceed. Dr. Hales hath showed them to many of our Nobility and from their general approbation of them, he thinks it very probable that a scheme for putting them in execution may take place next Winter.

I shall in a few days send by a friend who will call on Dr. Hales, all the materials which you was so obliging as to procure for me, and by the favour of the Doctor to draw up a Scheme from them for putting the Proposals in execution. My reason for deferring till now the sending them to the Doctor is that in one of his Letters he advised me not to print the Scheme as yet, lest the Gentlemen to whom it was shown might forget it by the time that they came to London. And had I applied to the Doctor as soon as I received them, I believe he might have thought me troublesome.

I am, with my Humble Service to Mrs. Baker,
Dear Sir, You ever obliged Humble Servant,

W. SHIPLEY

P.S. A few days since Alderman Locock,[3] a surgeon and Apothecary of this town brought me the enclosed worms with a letter. He thought if they were shown to the Royal Society with his account of them that it might vindicate Dr. Turner's account of worms similar to these, against Hill's scurrilous reflections on it.[4] I was in some doubt about sending them thinking it would be needless, being informed that Hill's reflections are so very low as to be far beneath the notice of the Society. But as the Case is very extraordinary, and the worms something different from those described by Dr. Turner, I thought, Sir, you might be willing to see them. The Alderman is a Gentleman of known veracity, and Thomas Green will if required make affidavit of the Fact. The Alderman desires to have them returned. In about a fortnight a Friend will call for them. I shall be much obliged, Sir, if you'll deliver to my Friend a few of your Wheel Animals if you can conveniently spare them, they are not to be found in this part of the Country. The Box had been sent last week but I was too late for the Carrier.

NOTES TO THE LETTERS

Letter I (Ryl. English MSS. 19, III, 154).

1 Robert Hooke (1635–1703), whose account of Kettering Stone was included in his *Micrographia*, published in 1665. An abridged edition of *Micrographia* had appeared in 1745. See R. T. Gunther, *Early Science in Oxford*, Vol. XIII (Oxford, 1938), p. 93.

2 Harsley was Sir Arthur Hesilrige Bt. (1704–63), a prominent inhabitant of Northampton. Hanborough was William Hanbury, F.R.S., of Kelmarsh, subsequently (1757) elected a member of the Society of Arts on Shipley's proposal. Jeykill was Joseph Jekyll of Dallington (d. 1752). Laughton was Charlewood Lawton, an original member of the Northampton Philosophical Society. (*Gentleman's Magazine*, Vol. XVI, 1746, p. 475; R.S.A., Sub. Bks.; information kindly supplied by Mr. P. I. King, County Archivist of Northampton.)

3 See below, Letter II, n. 2.

4 Mrs. Baker was Sophia, daughter of Daniel Defoe, whom
   Henry Baker had married in 1729 (*D.N.B.*). Parsons was
   James Parsons, M.D., F.R.S., F.S.A. (1705–70), Baker's
   intimate acquaintance and subsequently (1759) an
   influential member of the Society of Arts (J. Nichols,
   Literary Anecdotes of the Eighteenth Century, London,
   1812–15, Vol. V, p. 482; R.S.A., Sub. Bks.). Dr. Stuart
   is difficult to identify.

5 Peter Quenby (d. 1757), Sexton of All Saints' Parish
   Church, had a house in The Drapery, Northampton
   (information kindly supplied by Mr. D. Howard Halliday,
   Borough Librarian of Northampton).

6 See below, Letter II, n. 3.

Letter II (*Ryl. English MSS.* 19, III, 156).

1 The manuscript contains numerous alterations, corrections,
   and variant readings, especially in the opening paragraph,
   where the following crossed-out passage follows line 3:
   'Every Man that finds a Pleasure in examining and
   admiring the Works of his Creator must reap an
   additional Satisfaction if by any Means he can encourage
   or assist Others in Enquiries that tend to the same
   delightful Purpose, that of being acquainted with the
   wonderful Productions of Nature, and I should be a very
   undeserving Member of the Royal Society as well as
   greatly negligent of my own Happiness if I did not
   willingly embrace so fair an opportunity.'

2 In 1744 Baker had received the Copley Medal of the
   Royal Society for 'curious experiments relating to the
   crystallisation or configuration of the minute particles of
   saline bodies dissolved in a menstrum' (C. R. Weld,
   History of the Royal Society, London, 1948, Vol. I,
   p. 485 n.). He published his *Employment of the*

Microscope in 1753, part one of which was 'An Examination of Salts and Saline Substances'.

3 On 24th November 1747, Baker wrote a three-page letter to Doddridge expressing his appreciation of the honour of his correspondence, with a postscript: 'If Mr. Shipley is with you pray pay him my compliments.' (Ryl. English MSS. 19, III, 179, printed T. Stedman, *Letters to and from the Rev. Philip Doddridge*, Shrewsbury, 1790, pp. 408–15, and J. D. Humphreys, *Correspondence and Diary of Philip Doddridge*, Vol. V, London, 1831, pp. 24–30.)

Letter III (Ryl. English MSS. 19, III, 277–8; enclosed with 279, Doddridge to Baker, 11th May 1749)

1 John Cuff (*c.* 1708–72) was a scientific instrument maker who specialised in microscopes (see R. S. Clay and T. H. Court, *The History of the Microscope*, London, 1932, pp. 66–7, 122, 136 et sqq.).

2 Charlewood Lawton. See above Letter I, n. 2.

3 Richard Braifield (d. 1749), tanner and potter, had a house in The Drapery, Northampton (information kindly supplied by Mr. D. Howard Halliday, Borough Librarian of Northampton).

Letter IV (Ryl. English MSS. 19, III, 284).

1 See Letter I, n. 1.

2 Martin Folkes (1690–1754), President of the Royal Society, 1741–51 (see *D.N.B.*).

Letter V (Ryl. English MSS. 19, III, 289).

1 See the article on barometers in E. Chambers, *Cyclopædia or an Universal Dictionary of Arts and Sciences*, 2nd ed. (London, 1738) and 3rd ed. (London, 1751).

2 Baker visited Doddridge at his London home in August 1748 (see Letter from Dr. Doddridge to Mrs. Doddridge, 1st August 1748; New College, London, Doddridge MSS., made available through the courtesy of Dr. G. F. Nuttall).

Letter VI (*Ryl. English MSS.* 19, V, 50).

1 Shipley probably used Baron Stosch's copy of this famous gem (see Letter VII and J. H. Middleton, *The Engraved Gems of Classical Times*, Cambridge, 1891, p. xxiv).

2 David Erskine Baker (1730–67) and Henry Baker, Jun. (1734–66). See *D.N.B.*

Letter VII (*Ryl. English MSS.* 19, IV, 339).

1 Baron Phillipe von Stosch (1691–1756), a contemporary expert on antique gems. (See S. Reinach, *Pierres Gravées*, Paris, 1895, pp. 118–19; reference supplied through the courtesy of Mrs. Joan Martin of the Department of Coins and Medals, the British Museum.)

2 The Dublin Society for Improving Husbandry, Manufactures and other Useful Arts, founded in 1731. See *pp. 47–8*.

3 Stephen Hales, D.D., F.R.S. (1677–1761). See *pp. 47, 49–50*.

Letter VIII (*Ryl. English MSS.* 19, V, 301–3).

1 Shipley's interest in these antiquities may well have been stimulated by the publications of William Stukeley (1687–1765), notably *Stonehenge* (1740) and *Abury* (1743). Stukeley and Baker were fellow antiquaries. Baker communicated Shipley's descriptions to the Society of Antiquaries which returned thanks to them both (Society of Antiquaries of London, Minutes, 17th January 1754).

2 John Wall, M.D. (1708–76), eminent physician of Worcester,

philanthropist and amateur artist. See T. R. Nash, *Collections for the History of Worcestershire* (London, 1792), Vol. II, p. 126.

3 Henry Locock, an apothecary who served as Mayor of Northampton in 1749 (information kindly supplied by Mr. D. Howard Halliday, Borough Librarian of Northampton).

4 Daniel Turner, M.D. (1710–48), contributed a paper on 'Two cases of insects voided by the urinary passages' to the Royal Society's *Philosophical Transactions*, Vol. XXXIII (1724–5), p. 410. On 18th September 1753, Baker wrote about the matter to William Arderon, his Norwich correspondent, calling it 'a Case very extraordinary; but the Truth, I think, I need not doubt' (Victoria and Albert Museum, Forster Collection, Arderon-Baker Correspondence, I, 99). 'Sir' John Hill (*c.* 1716–75), a former friend of Baker, turned against him after his (Hill's) rejection as a Fellow of the Royal Society. Hill's *Review of the Works of the Royal Society* (London, 1751, pp. 59–60) contained an attack on Turner's paper. Subsequently Hill was also rejected as a member of the Society of Arts (see Trueman Wood, p. 46).

[4]

MINUTES OF THE FIRST MEETING OF THE SOCIETY OF ARTS

Rawthmell's Coffee House, Henrietta Street, Covent Garden, 22nd March 1754.[1] At a Meeting of some Noblemen, Clergy,[2] Gentlemen, and Merchants, in order to form a Society for the Encouragement of Arts, Manufactures and Commerce in Great Britain.

It was proposed to consider, whether a Reward should not be given for the finding of Cobalt in this Kingdom; as there is Reason to believe it may be discovered here, if diligently sought after.

And as Arsenic Smalt and Zaffer are prepared from Cobalt, and all we use of these is imported from foreign parts, Mr. Shipley (who acted as Secretary) was desired to search the Books of Entries at the Custom House, to learn what Quantities of each are annually imported, and to make his Report at the next meeting.

It was also proposed to consider whether a Reward should not be given for the Cultivation of Madder in this Kingdom.

In consequence whereof, the Secretary was desired to enquire what Quantities of Madder are annually imported; and the Gentlemen present were likewise desired to inform themselves, wherefore the cultivation thereof has been neglected in this Kingdom, and whether it is a great Impoverisher of Lands?[3]

It was likewise proposed, to consider of giving Rewards for the Encouragement of Boys and Girls in the Art of Drawing, and it being the opinion of all present that the Art of Drawing is absolutely necessary in many Employments, Trades and Manufactures, and that the Encouragement thereof may prove of great Utility to the Public, it was resolved to bestow Premiums on a certain number of Boys or Girls under the Age of Sixteen, who shall produce the best Pieces of Drawing, and Show themselves most capable, when properly examined.

The farther Consideration of these proposals was referred to the next Meeting, and after directing that a Book of Rates be bought for the Use of the Society, the Company adjourned to Friday next, March 29th.

At this Meeting were present the Right Honble. Lord Viscount Folkestone, the Right Honble. Lord Romney, the Rev. Dr. Stephen Hales, John Goodchild Esq., Messrs. Lawrence, Baker, Crisp, Brander, Short, Messiter, and Shipley.[4]

[5]

FIRST NOTICE PUBLISHED BY THE SOCIETY OF ARTS

To the PUBLICK

London [25 March] 1754[5]

Some of the Nobility, Clergy, Gentlemen, and Merchants, having at heart the Good of their Country, have lately met together, in order to form a Society for the Encouragement of Arts, Manufactures and Commerce, in *Great-Britain*: by Bestowing Rewards, from Time to Time, for such Productions, Inventions, or Improvements, as shall tend to the Employing of the Poor, to the Increase of Trade, and to the Riches and Honour of this Kingdom, by promoting Industry and Emulation: And, though at present their Plan is not complete, it has nevertheless been resolved to make a Beginning in Manner following: That is to say,

COBALT[6] having been already discovered in some Parts of this Kingdom—For producing Specimens, not less than ten Pounds in Weight, for the best in Quality, to be produced on or before the 15th Day of *January* next, with satisfactory Certificates of the Place where found, and reasonable Assurances that it may be obtained in Quantity, £30—To be determined that Day fortnight.

For raising and curing the most and best MADDER for Dying in this Kingdom, not less than twenty Pounds Weight, of which Samples to be shewn, with satisfactory Certificates, on or before the 15th Day of *January*, in the Year 1756, £30—To be determined that Day Fortnight.[7]

For the best DRAWING by Boys and Girls under the Age of 14 Years, and Proof of their Abilities, on or before the 15th Day of *January*, 1755, £15.

Likewise for the best DRAWINGS by Boys and Girls, between the Age of Fourteen and Seventeen, with like Proof of their Abilities, on or before the same Day, £15.

By Order of the SUBSCRIBERS,

WILLIAM SHIPLEY

Note, Any Information or Advice that may forward this Design for the publick Good, will be received thankfully, and duly considered, if communicated by Letter directed to Mr. *Shipley*, at Mr. *Messiter's*, Surgeon, in *Great Pulteney-street, near Golden-square, London.*

NOTES TO THE MINUTES AND NOTICE

1 Two versions of these minutes exist: (i) the so-called 'Rough Book' in Shipley's own handwriting, and (ii) the version transcribed by John Champion for Volume I of the official series of Society Minute Books. Both (i) and (ii) originally entered 'January' instead of March, and in (i) Shipley put '1753' instead of '1754'. Evidently he was still unaccustomed to the reformed calendar though it was by this time eighteen months old.

2 'Clergy' added as an afterthought by Shipley in (i).

3 'of Land' in (i).

4 In (i) Shipley's name comes before Crisp's, Baker's and Brander's.

5 The text of this notice was approved on 25th March 1754, and 'Ordered to be published in some of the Daily and Evening Papers three times a Week for a Month afterwards at proper Intervals' (Soc. Min., Rough Book).

6 On Shipley's recommendation a note explaining the appearance of cobalt was added to the notice 'that the Common People might have a chance for our promised Premium'. Baker composed the note, which was included

in the version of the notice published on 15th June,
though the minutes report it as having been approved on
the 19th June (Soc. Min.).

7 For the purpose of these awards for dyestuffs, see Hudson
and Luckhurst, pp. 8, 89–90, 96–7.

[6]

THE 'PLAN' OF THE SOCIETY OF ARTS, 1755*

WHEREAS the Riches, Honour, Strength and Prosperity of a
Nation depend in a great Measure on the Knowledge and
Improvement of useful Arts, Manufactures, Etc. several of
the Nobility and Gentry of this Kingdom, being fully sensible
that due Encouragements and Rewards are greatly conducive
to excite a Spirit of Emulation and Industry, have resolved to
form themselves into a Society, by the Name of *The Society for
the Encouragement of Arts, Manufactures and Commerce*, by
bestowing Premiums for such Productions, Inventions, or
Improvements, as shall tend to the employing of the Poor,
and the Increase of Trade.

And as all Communities must be established under certain
Regulations, it is thought necessary for the orderly Dispatch
of Business in this Society, that there be one President, four
Vice-Presidents, a Treasurer, and a Secretary; to be elected by
Ballot, on the first *Wednesday* in *March* annually.

And whereas the Right Honourable *Jacob* Lord Viscount
Folkestone, being unanimously requested, has been pleased to
accept the Office of President; the Right Honourable *Robert*
Lord *Romney*, being also unanimously requested, has been
pleased to accept the Office of Vice-President; the Rev. Dr.
Stephen Hales, Charles Whitworth, and *James Theobald*, Esqrs.

* See *p. 57*.

have unanimously been elected Vice-Presidents; *John Good-child*, Esq. Treasurer; and Mr. *William Shipley*, Secretary: Each of them to continue in his respective Office until the first *Wednesday* in *March*, 1756, when a new Election of Officers shall be made: Any seven or more of the subscribing Members, shall, for the Time to come, elect Persons into this Society by Ballot, who have been regularly proposed, by giving in their Names in writing at a preceding Meeting.

There shall be four General Meetings of this Society in every Year, within the Bills of Mortality, *viz.* On the Second *Wednesday* in *December*, the Third *Wednesday* in *January*, the First *Wednesday* in *March*, (which is the Day of the Election of Officers) and the First *Wednesday* in *April*; and also as many other Meetings as the President, a Vice-President, or five or more of the said Society shall appoint. And at the general Meetings, (but not at any other Meetings) if seven Members at the least be present (whereof the President or a Vice-President always be one) they shall have full Power to make Rules and Orders for the good Government of the said Society: to be valid and take Place, provided the same be confirmed at some succeeding General Meeting, where seven at least of the Members shall be present, the President or a Vice-President being one: And the same Method shall be observed in the altering or repealing any Rules or Orders that have been so made and confirmed.

And at all general and other Meetings, if the President be absent, the Vice-President then present, first named in the List of Vice-Presidents, shall be Chairman of the said Meeting; and in Case the President and all the Vice-Presidents shall be absent, any Five or more shall appoint one of the Members then present to preside for that Time.

And whereas the Intent and Purpose of this Society is to encourage Ingenuity and Industry, by bestowing of Premiums on the most deserving the Expence of which must be defrayed by the voluntary Contributions of its Members; no Person shall be deemed a Member until he shall have paid Two Guineas (or such larger Sum as he thinks proper) for the first Year. And every Person shall continue to pay Two Guineas (or what more he pleases) annually, so long as he shall be willing to continue a Member of this Society. But whosoever shall at once pay down Twenty Guineas (or more) in lieu of all Contributions, shall be a Member during his Life. And as the Good the Society can do, will be in Proportion to the Rewards it is able to bestow, all occasional Benefactions or Donations from any Person or Persons whatever, will be thankfully received by the Society: And fair Accounts in Writing shall be kept of all Receipts, Payments, and other Transactions of the said Society, and of its Officers and Agents, to be viewed and inspected by any Subscriber or Benefactor, upon Occasion: For the Examination, auditing and subscribing of which Accounts, a Committee shall be appointed, annually, on the Third *Wednesday* in *January*; which Committee shall make their Report to the general Meeting on the First *Wednesday* in *March*: and that before they proceed to the Election of their Officers.

And as the proposing proper Subjects for Encouragement, and the Distribution of Rewards with the strictest Impartiality and Justice, are what this Society most earnestly wishes and desires: and in order to effect the same, it seems absolutely necessary, to consult with such Person or Persons as are best able to judge of, or discover the Truth or Value of any Matter or Thing offered or proposed to this Society: It shall therefore be allowable for any Member thereof, with Leave of the Society, to introduce, at the general, or other Meetings, any such Person or Persons as he shall think capable of giving some useful Information, Assistance, or Advice.

Foreigners, or Persons that do not usually reside in *Great Britain*, may be elected, by Ballot, to be corresponding Members of this Society, without being subject to Contributions: And if they happen to come to *London*, shall be admitted to the Meetings of the Society, but shall have no Right to vote, unless they become Contributors.

If Differences of Opinion should arise concerning Matters or Things brought before this Society, a Ballot, if demanded, shall in all such Cases determine the Resolution of the said Society: and if the Votes be equal, the President, or Vice-President, or presiding Member, shall give the casting Vote.

And if the President shall happen to die or resign, in such Case a new President shall be elected, at the next General Meeting of the Society, by a Majority of the Members then present, provided their Number is not less than seven, whereof a Vice-President shall be one: And until such President shall be so elected, the first Vice-President in Nomination, present at any Meeting, shall preside. And if any Vice-President shall die or resign, seven or more of the Members of this Society, (the President or a surviving Vice-President being one) shall in like Manner elect a new Vice-President.

Finally, In all Matters this Society shall be directed and governed by such Rules and Orders, as, from Time to Time, shall for that Purpose be made, confirmed, and established. *London, Feb. 19, 1755*

[7]

SHIPLEY'S FIRST LETTER TO BENJAMIN FRANKLIN*

Craig's Court September the 13th, 1755

Sir,

I believe that you will be surprised to hear from one who

* American Philosophical Society MSS., Franklin Papers, Vol. I, 1, No. 38; printed L. W. Labaree, ed., *The Papers of Benjamin Franklin*, Vol. VI, New Haven, 1963, pp. 186–9.

am an entire Stranger and living at so great a distance; but as I have often heard so great a Character of your Ingenuity and extensive Public-Spirited Benevolence I shall mention no more by way of Apology for troubling you on this occasion, than that your Plan for promoting of Useful knowledge among the British Plantations in America, was sent me some time ago by Dr. Alexander Garden of South Carolina Physician which I as Secretary to the Premium Society in London communicated to Many of our Members at our next Board after I received it;[1] it was highly approved by all present, several of whom said that they thought we should be very happy in having you for one of our correspondent Members; for they thought that a Gentleman of your extensive general Knowledge will be able to give us Intelligence of Many things of Importance that may be encouraged by Premiums to many of our Plantations in America, therefore with a View that I hope that you will make one of our body I have enclosed one of our Plans,[2] a Hand bill and also a List of our Subscribers. By the two former you will be able to make a Judgment of what are our designs in General, and have been last Year in particular, and by the latter you will see our Infant Strength. Although we are so considerable a Body we have not been a Society more than Eight Months, it is expected that we shall soon be incorporated and perhaps may have grants from Parliament sufficient to promote by Premiums Things of the Uttermost Public Utility.[3]

It is true in Great Britain so many Improvements have been already made that some have thought a Scheme of this kind is here quite Needless but we find that here is still a Boundless Field for Improvements in many Arts Manufactures, and other Articles which may in time prove of the Uttmost consequence to this Kingdom, therefore I believe that you will think our Plan far from being any ways Chimerical but on the Contrary that the Design of it is truely laudable.

Our Premiums will perhaps be often offered for promoting

Articles of Importance in our Plantations in America which on account of their being Younger in Arts and Manufactures than Great Britain consequently there is more room there than with us for Improvements.

Doctor Alexander Garden has lately sent us a list of many Articles which he thinks may be successfully promoted by Premiums in Carolina for which I am desired to write him a Letter of Thanks from our Society, and to acknowledge the great Favour that he did us.[4]

Amongst the many Articles which he mentions as proper to be promoted are 1 The Cultivation of Vines 2 Sesamune 3 Gossipium 4 Mulberry Trees 5 Cochineal 6 Hemp and Flax 7 making Potash etc.

All which will next year be taken into Consideration by our Society and by Premiums as far promoted as our Fund will enable us, and any Articles which you think may be success fully and properly promoted by Premiums in Philadelphia, if communicated, the Favour will be equally acknowledged.

In regard to your well calculated and most extensive Public Spirited Plan,[5] which I hope [ere] long to see in Execution, I believe the design of our Society may very well concurr with it; for I perceive from what has been already effected that we shall be a means of bringing to light things of the Utmost Importance to this Community.

Should I mention the new Inventions and Improvements in Navigation, Husbandry, and Manufactures which have been already communicated to us they would perhaps exceed your belief; should you see some Models of our Machines for Improving Manufactures, you would I believe allow that the Contrivances were so very new and extraordinary that you would almost think them the products of more than human Inventions. I make no doubt but if your plan was in Execution in America and a Correspondence Carried on with ours and many other Societies in Great Britain that it would occasion such a Circulation of most useful and Beneficial Knowledge as might exceed our warmest Expectations.

Should you be willing Sir to comply with this my Respect [sic] in favouring us with your Correspondence an Account of all particulars relating to our affairs shall be sent you, or should you be willing to honour the List of our corresponding Members with your Name I hope Sir That you will let me have the credit of proposing you for a Member. By our Plan you will perceive Sir that our Correspondent Members are liable to no Expences whatever. I hope Sir when Opportunity Serves you will favour me with your Answer.[6] I am,

Sir,
Your most obedient humble Servant
WILLIAM SHIPLEY

NOTES TO THE LETTER

1 Soc. Min., 18th June 1755.

2 See *pp.* 192–5.

3 Shipley was over-optimistic in his forecast of a Charter and a Parliamentary grant. The Society was not incorporated until 1847 and received no funds from the legislature.

4 See *pp.* 59–60.

5 Franklin's *Proposal for Promoting Useful Knowledge among the British Plantations in America* (Philadelphia, 1743) was the foundation document of the American Philosophical Society. (See Labaree, op. cit., Vol. II, pp. 378–83.)

6 Franklin replied accepting corresponding membership, though he insisted on contributing to the fund, on 27th November 1755 (G.B. I., No. 126, printed Labaree, op. cit., Vol. VI, pp. 275–7; Soc. Min., 1st September 1756).

[8]

SHIPLEY'S LETTERS OF RESIGNATION
(R.S.A., L.A., D.9/4-5)

I   Shipley to the Society of Arts

October the 1st, 1760

Gentlemen,

Having lately engaged in Business of such Importance as to render me incapable of discharging my Duty to this Society as their Register, without very much injuring my own Affairs; I take this Method to inform you of my Intentions to resign my Office as Register; but though it will not suit me to serve you any longer in that Station, I shall on every Occasion use my utmost Endeavours to promote the Interest of this Society as a Member thereof, and I acknowledge most gratefully the many Favours you have for several Years conferred upon me, who remain with the greatest Respect

Gentlemen,

Your most obedient, and very humble Servant,

WILLIAM SHIPLEY

II   Same to the same

Strand Decr. the 10th 1760

Gentlemen,

Having (pursuant to your Orders) delivered to my Successor Mr. Tuckwell all the Articles belonging to the Society which have been by you committed to my Trust, and on this Occasion I most gratefully acknowledge the Favour you have done me in continuing me so long your Register and more particularly for your accepting of my imperfect Service[s] which have often been so very defective as rather to deserve your Censure than your unanimous Thanks.

It is with the utmost Pleasure that I can congratulate you on your great success in your most noble and Public spirited Undertakings for the Good of Mankind in General and of this Nation in Particular. With what Joy do I behold your Plan patronised by such Numbers of the Nobility and Gentry. As you are in so short a Time increased to no middle Degree of Greatness and as there [are] amongst you such a Multitude of Gentlemen profoundly skilled in every Branch of Beneficial Knowledge I presume that there will be no Sums how great soever contributed to this Society but you will soon find Subjects proper to employ them, and I presage from the un-bounded Flow of Public spirited Benevolence which every where prevails throughout this Kingdom that there are no Designs how great soever which you will propose to be executed but sufficient Sums will soon be raised for you properly to promote them.

As my Abilities are so small I despair even of contributing my Mite towards promoting your so great and Good Designs, but you have ever my best Wishes which are that your Successes in all your Undertakings for the Public Good may be equal to that Noble and Public spirited Zeal by which on every Occasion you have so remarkably distinguished yourselves and, with the utmost Respect, I subscribe myself

Gentlemen,

Your most obedient

and very humble Servant,

WILLIAM SHIPLEY

[9]

SHIPLEY'S PLAN TO EXTEND THE MAIDSTONE SOCIETY, 1786

A
PROPOSAL
TO ESTABLISH
A SOCIETY,
FOR
PROMOTING USEFUL KNOWLEDGE
IN THE
COUNTY OF KENT.
ADDRESSED TO THE
INHABITANTS OF THE SAID COUNTY

The improvement of agriculture and the arts, has ever been esteemed an object of the greatest importance to the prosperity of a people. But improvements of every kind advance slowly, and without public encouragement, ingenuity is apt to suppress its talents and invention to conceal its experiments. To call forth, patronise, and reward the exertions of individuals for the general advantage of the community, to record and recommend their successful labours, and to make the discoveries of a few the property of all, was, and is the generous design of that truly patriotic institution the Society of Arts. It need not be said, that from the efforts of this liberal Society, more solid benefits have been derived to our country, within the short space of thirty years, than from all the improvements that have been made throughout this kingdom in half a century before that time.

From the example and in aid of this excellent institution, whose views extend over the whole British empire; similar

Associations upon a more limited plan have been formed, conducted with much spirit, and happily rewarded with success. In the year 1756, a Society for improving Agriculture was first established in Brecknockshire,[1] where such considerable advances have been made, that large tracts of land which before were only worth half-a-crown an acre are now let for twelve shillings. Establishments of the like sort have since arisen in Yorkshire, Norfolk, Somersetshire, Lancashire, and Hampshire.[2] All these County Societies still subsist and flourish. And wherever they have been formed, Agriculture has been carried on to greater perfection, new species of productions introduced, moors and fens drained and cultivated, new inventions for the shortening of labour devised and adopted, and both individuals and the public benefited. The obvious advantages to a country derived from such institutions have not escaped the observations of foreigners. So striking are they to the watchful inhabitants of the neighbouring nations, that in several of their provinces they have in imitation of what has been done in Great Britain and Ireland, formed such societies.[3]

Some of the Nobility, Clergy, Gentlemen, Merchants, and Tradesmen, have for some time past formed a Society for introducing useful knowledge into Maidstone and its environs. Their principal intentions have been to promote improvements in agriculture, in all its branches; but as their plan was so very extensive, as to take in improvements of any and every kind, provided they are useful, and tend to the benefit of the public, they have therefore directed their enquiries to various other subjects besides agriculture; as to Mechanics, Household Oeconomy, in several of its branches; and to many other articles, which need not here be mentioned.

Nor have objects of humanity escaped their notice. For it is well known, what this Society did in the beginning of the year 1783, towards putting a stop to a most malignant fever which then raged in Maidstone gaol. More than seventy of the prisoners were infected with it, fifteen of whom died in a short time. The said Society first set on foot a subscription, to carry on very expensive processes, which were judged to be necessary, to eradicate so dreadful a distemper. By its timely exertions a subscription was raised amounting to £351 10s. with which money the medical gentlemen of the Society were enabled to direct several very costly experiments to be tried upon the prisoners, and also to purify the air in the wards of the gaol; and the whole of these processes were so judiciously ordered, and punctually carried into execution, that the disorder was soon perfectly cured. For this service its members received public thanks from the Grand Jury and Judges of Assize.

Many are the important objects which the Members of this Society have in view; for the heads of which the reader is referred to a list of the desiderata, inserted on the other side. One advantage which the public may reasonably expect to reap from a society for promoting improvements in agriculture, &c. is, besides the profits that will arise to the owners of the land, the introducing much new employment for the poor: which will tend to reduce the poor rates, and also make many of them much better members of the community than they are at present. The inhabitants of the county of Kent have, for several ages past, been the greatest improvers of agriculture of any others in this kingdom. They first introduced the cultivation of apples, cherries and hops; sainfoin, lucerne, and some other valuable grasses amongst us; and by their ingenuity and public spirit the woollen, silk, paper, thread, and some other valuable manufactures were first established, amongst us; and this nation is greatly indebted to them for the eminent services they have done to their country by the improvements they have made in various other branches of useful knowledge. This county is better formed by nature than perhaps any other in the kingdom for such an institution, not only on account of its nearness to the metropolis, but also for the great conveniences it has for sending heavy or bulky goods to London by water, as it is more than two parts in three surrounded by the sea and the Thames, has many navigable rivers, and there are but few places within the same from whence goods may not soon be carried to some port or navigable river, and sent to London by water; there is also in this county a very great variety of hill and vale, and a vast number of different soils, most of which are capable of being much improved. Therefore as a proposal is now made, which, if properly encouraged will be a means of diffusing beneficial knowledge, method and custom to every part of this province, it is not to be doubted, but the inhabitants, in general, will be as ready to *cultivate* useful knowledge amongst them, as their forefathers have been in former ages assiduous to *plant* it: and particularly when they consider, how very easy it is for a set of public spirited gentlemen and others, to carry such a design into execution, and that plans similar to this, have already been long since formed, in several counties of this kingdom, and carried into execution in a very extensive manner; and that the places where they were established, have been by them greatly improved, and the whole has been effected with but a very small expence to the members of such societies as individuals. Therefore it is not doubted but many public spirited gentlemen, and ladies,[4] merchants, tradesmen, farmers and others, will readily join in promoting this Society, now in its infant state; as its plan is calculated to forward every undertaking of public utility; and that they will desire to have its Influence extended to every part of this county. It is hoped by their subscriptions they will enable the Society to reward public spirited or beneficial undertakings, whenever they meet them; that whoever shall make the most considerable progress in any branch of beneficial knowledge, or exhibit to the Society the most improved performance in any species of mechanic skill or contrivance;

whoever shall introduce, execute, or cause to be executed any new method or contrivance that is calculated for the real interest, credit, embellishment, or in time of distress, for the relief of this county, or any considerable part thereof, may receive a reward suitable to the merit of his or her services.[5]

The Members, therefore, of the Society established for promoting useful knowledge in Maidstone and its environs, intend to extend their plan, and hereby propose to take in the whole county of Kent, altering their title of the *Society*, for promoting useful knowledge in Maidstone and its environs, to that of the *Kentish Society*, for promoting useful knowledge throughout the county of Kent. When this is become a County Society, it is hoped that its Members will be as numerous as they are in other County Societies in several parts of this kingdom. For it is presumed many of the worthy inhabitants of Kent, (the earliest civilised and first cultivated part of Britain) when they consider from whom they are descended, will endeavour to imitate the ingenuity and public spirit of their forefathers, and think it inglorious to be themselves inactive when their native county humbly requests their assistance.

A list *of the* DESIDERATA *of the* KENTISH SOCIETY, *or of those Articles which they desire to promote*

As Human Culture is much more deserving the patronage of the Society, than the breeding of cattle and Poultry, or the culture of vegetables; as human beings, who are endued with reason, are preferable to beasts, birds, trees and plants; therefore the Society intend first to try to promote by their pecuniary rewards or honorary gratifications, any improvements in the Plans of Education calculated for the Instruction of Children in Charity Schools; such rewards will also be given to them who shall establish, promote, or improve Sunday Schools; for such institutions, it is presumed, will very much tend to check vice amongst some of the most ignorant and abandoned of the lower class of people; therefore, in a political view, such institutions deserve the greatest patronage from the Society. The other articles intended to be promoted are as follows:

In AGRICULTURE

Cattle, new and useful sorts to introduce, also of sheep and swine.
Poultry, new and useful breeds.
Fruit trees for orchards, new and valuable sorts.
Seeds and plants for gardens, new and useful sorts.
Trees and shrubs, new and valuable sorts.
Implements in husbandry and gardening, new and useful sorts.
Manures, new and useful sorts.

HOUSHOLD OECONOMY

Water to soften, and a substitute for yeast.
Cheap and wholesome food, for the benefit of the poor.
Coffee of English materials.
Flesh meat, to preserve without salt.
Oil and ink, to discharge from clothes, boards, or furniture.
Sea coal, to burn to advantage.
Soap, a cheap substitute for.
Vermin, to kill, as rats, bugs, &c.
Wines of various sorts, to make.
Impure air, to correct.
Employment for the poor, new methods of which several they have in view, and many other articles too numerous to be inserted.

. . . . .

[A list of names of members of the Society will be found reprinted from this pamphlet on *pp.* 226–7.]

It is proposed that an annual subscription of any sum, not less than one guinea, shall entitle a person to be a Member; and the names of all persons who give annual benefactions, not less than half a guinea, shall be published with the list of Members.

As soon as a convenient number of subscribers have joined the Society, a plan for its regulation will be printed, and also their transactions will be occasionally published, and sent to all the Members.

Subscriptions are taken in by Mr. Shipley, Maidstone; the Rev. Mr. Parsons, of Wye; Mr. James Six, of Canterbury; Mr. John Latham, Surgeon, at Dartford; Mr. Henry Creed, at Ashford;

By order of the Society.

W. SHIPLEY, Treasurer

N.B. Any Information or advice that may forward the Designs of this Society for the Public good, will be received thankfully and duly considered if communicated by Letter, directed to Mr. Shipley, in Maidstone, Kent.

NOTES TO THE PLAN TO EXTEND THE MAIDSTONE SOCIETY

1 This was the Society established by Charles Powell, see *p.* 61.
2 There had been an agricultural society at Doncaster since 1769, in Norfolk since 1774, at Bath since 1777, at Manchester since 1777, and at Odiham since 1783. (See Lord Ernle, *English Farming past and present*, London, 5th ed. 1936, p. 209; W. Bowden, *Industrial Society in England towards the end of the eighteenth century*, pp. 46–7; and *Jnl. R.S.A.*, Vol. CVIII, 1960, pp. 770–1.)

3 For the numerous French agricultural societies founded
   between 1757 and 1789, see A. J. Bourde, *The Influence
   of England on the French Agronomes* (Cambridge, 1953),
   p. 195; Shipley kept a newspaper cutting reporting the
   premiums given by the Society at Valladolid in 1780
   (M.M., Shipley's Memo Bk., f. 57). Other continental
   societies based on the English model were the Patriotic
   Society of Hamburg and the Free Economic Society of
   St. Petersburg, both founded in 1765 (see J. A. Prescott,
   'The Russian Free, Imperial, Economic Society,
   1765–1917', *Jnl. R.S.A.*, CXII, 1965, pp. 33–7; *Die
   Patriotische Gesellschaft zu Hamburg, 1765–1965*,
   Festschrift published by the Society, 1965).

4 Compare the 'Scheme' of 1753 (see *p.* 44).

5 Compare the 'Proposals' of 1753 (see *p.* 43).

LISTS AND TABLES

[1]

LIST OF LETTERS BETWEEN SHIPLEY AND CHARLES WHITWORTH, 1755, PRESERVED IN GUARD BOOKS AND LOOSE ARCHIVES OF THE SOCIETY OF ARTS

DATE (in 1755)	AUTHOR	SUBJECT	REFERENCE
(1) 6th June:	W. to S.:	Tells S. he has already seen plan of the Society:	G.B. I, 11.
(2) 24th June:	S. to W.:	Buff leather and Dr. Garden:	L.A. (M.), A1/25
(3) 1st July:	W. to S.:	Thanks for (2):	G.B. I, 31
(4) 15th July:	S. to W.:	Dr. Garden's observation:	Ibid, III, 19
(5) 22nd July:	S. to W.:	Little news:	L.A. (M.), A1/27
(6) 31st July:	W. to S.:	Dr. Garden:	G.B. I, 35
(7) 7th Aug.:	S. to W.:	Dean Tucker:	L.A. (M.), A1/30
(8) 14th Aug.:	S. to W.:	Chas. Powell's scheme:	G.B. III, 20
(9) 15th Aug.:	W. to S.:	„	Ibid, I, 44.
(10) 24th Aug.:	W. to S.:	„	Ibid, I, 46
(11) 1st Sept.:	W. to S.:	„	Ibid, I, 49
(12) 1st Sept.:	W. to S.: (Private letter)	„	Ibid, I, 50
(13) 6th Sept.:	S. to W.:	„	Ibid, III, 22
(14) 9th Sept.:	S. to W. (with W.'s reply):	„	Ibid, III, 24
(15) 15th Sept.:	W. to S.:	„	Ibid, I, 53
(16) 24th Sept.:	W. to S.:	Colonial correspondence:	Ibid, I, 54
(17) 10th Oct.:	W. to S.:	Procedure at Society's Meetings:	Ibid, I, 58
(18) 2nd Nov.:	W. to S.:	Procedure at Society's Meetings:	Ibid, I, 63

[2]

PUPILS AT SHIPLEY'S SCHOOL, 1753–61

* The initial letters stand for the following sources: D=R. Dossie, *Memoirs of Agriculture*, Vol. III, London (1782); E=E. Edwards, *Anecdotes of Painters* (London, 1808); G=T. J. Mulvany, *Life of Gandon* (Dublin, 1846); J=T. Jones, 'Memoirs', *Walpole Society*, Vol. XXXII (London, 1951); S=J. T. Smith, *Nollekens and His Times* (London, 1828).

COSWAY, RICHARD (1742–1821)	Miniature and portrait painter. Premiums 1755, '57, '58, '59, '60. R.A. 1771. (D*; J; S)
CROSSE, RICHARD (1742–1810)	Miniature painter. Premium 1758. Painter in enamel to The King, 1790. (J)
GANDON, JAMES (1742–1823)	Architect. Premiums 1757, '58, '59, '62. R.A. Gold Medallist for architecture, 1769. (G)
GRESSE, JOHN ALEXANDER (1740–94)	Water colour painter. Premiums 1755, '56, '57, '58, '59, '61, '62. Drawing master to the daughters of King George III, 1777. (D)
GROSSE, FRANCIS (1731–91)	Antiquarian and amateur artist. (G)
HENDERSON, JOHN (1747–85)	Engraver and successful actor. Premium 1762. (G)
HODGES, WILLIAM (1744–97)	Landscape painter. Premiums 1759, '62. R.A. 1787. (E)
HUMPHRY, OZIAS (1742–1810)	Miniature and portrait painter. R.A. 1791. (J)
KITCHINGHAM, JOHN (1740?–81)	Miniature, portrait and seascape painter. Premium 1762. R.A. Exhibitor from 1770. (D)
MARSDEN, BARBARA	Under 12 in 1755. Premiums 1755, '56, '57, '58. (D)

MORTIMER, JOHN HAMILTON (1741–79)	History painter. Premiums 1759, '60, '61. A.R.A. 1778. (S)
NOLLEKENS, JOSEPH (1737–1823)	Sculptor. Premiums 1759, '60, '61. R.A. 1772. (S)
PARRY, WILLIAM (1742–91)	Portrait painter. Premiums 1760, '61. A.R.A. 1722. (E)
PARS, WILLIAM (1742–82)	Portrait painter. Premiums 1756, '57, '58, '59, '60, '61. Premiums A.R.A. 1770. (J)
PORTER, JOHN ASHWOOD	Son of a drawing master in Wapping. Premium 1755. (D)
ROBERTSON, GEORGE (1748?–88)	Landscape painter. Premiums, 1760, '61. Celebrated for his views of Jamaica. (D)
SMART, JOHN (1740–1811)	Miniature painter. Premiums, 1755, '56, '57, '58. Worked for some time in India. (D)
SMITH, NATHANIEL (1741?–after 1800)	Sculptor. Premiums 1758, '59, '60, '61. Assistant to Joseph Nollekens (*q.v. supra*). (S)
TAYLOR, SIMON (1743?–72?)	Botanical painter. Premiums 1756, '57, '58, '59, '61. Engaged by Lord Bute to paint live plants at Kew. (E)
WHEATLEY, FRANCIS (1747–1801)	Portrait and landscape painter. Premiums 1762, '63, R.A. 1791. (E)
WILLIS, WILLIAM (b. 1746?)	Glass ornament cutter. Premium 1759. (D)

[3]

SUBSEQUENT CAREERS OF SHIPLEY'S PUPILS

* Society of Arts premium winner.
† Winner of premium for textile patterns.

ARCHITECT
James Gandon*†
AMATEUR ARTIST
Francis Grosse
BOTANICAL DRAUGHTSMAN
Simon Taylor*†
ENGRAVER
John Henderson
(later an actor)
GLASS ORNAMENT CUTTER
William Willis*†
HISTORY PAINTER
J. H. Mortimer*
LANDSCAPE PAINTER
J. A. Gresse*
William Hodges*
George Robertson*

PORTRAIT PAINTER
William Pars*†
William Parry*
Francis Wheatley*
PORTRAIT AND MINIATURE PAINTER
Richard Cosway*
Richard Crosse*
Ozias Humphry
John Kitchingham*
John Smart*
SCULPTOR
Joseph Nollekens*
Nathaniel Smith*
SUBSEQUENT CAREER UNKNOWN
Barbara Marsden*†
(married another artist)
J. A. Porter*

[4]

SHIPLEY'S PUPILS AS WINNERS OF THE
SOCIETY'S PREMIUMS FOR POLITE ARTS, 1755–61

* Drawing preserved by the Society. † See illustrations.

1755 'For the best Drawings by Boys and Girls under the Age of
14':
1st: Richard Cosway: *Head of one of the Vertues expressing
compassion*, in chalks
2nd: John Smart: *An Academy figure*, in pencil*

3rd: J. A. Gresse: *An Old Warrior's Head*, in chalks*

4th: Barbara Marsden: *A Cottage surrounded by Trees*, in Indian ink*†

5th: J. A. Porter: *Boaz and the Servant set over the Reapers*, pencil and ink outline*

1756 'For the best Drawings by Boys and Girls under the Age of 14':

1st: John Smart: *Human figure starting from a rising serpent*, in pencil*

2nd: William Pars: *A Head of Laocoon*, in chalks

4th Simon Taylor: *The Head of a Rabbi*; pen and ink

5th: Barbara Marsden *The Head of an Old Woman*, black and red chalk

'For the best Drawings by Boys and Girls under the Age of 17':

2nd: J. A. Gresse: *An Academy Figure*, drawing

'For the most ingenious and best fancied Designs, proper for Weavers, Embroiderers, or Calico Printers; drawn by Boys or Girls under the Age of 17':

4th: William Pars*†

1757 'For the best Drawings by Boys under the Age of 14':

1st: William Pars: *An Academy Figure*, in chalks

'For the best Drawings by Boys under the Age of 17':

1st: John Smart: *Portrait of Mr. William Shipley*, in chalks

2nd: Simon Taylor: *Landscape with Cattle*, in black pencil

3rd: James Gandon: *An Academy Figure*, in chalks*

'For the most ingenious and best fancied Designs . . . proper for Weavers, Embroiderers or Calico-Printers drawn by Boys under the Age of 17':

2nd: Richard Cosway

3rd: J. A. Gresse*†

'For the most ingenious and best fancied Designs . . . proper for Weavers [etc.] . . . drawn by Girls under the Age of 17':

1st: Barbara Marsden

1758 'For the best drawings of an Human Figure in plaster by Boys and Girls under the Age of 18' (general subject: *The Dancing Faun*):

1st: John Smart*
2nd: Richard Cosway
3rd: J. A. Gresse*
4th: William Pars*
'For the best Drawings of an Human Figure after a print, by Boys under the Age of 16' (general subject: *The Farnesian Hercules*, to be done in chalks):
4th: Simon Taylor*
5th: Richard Crosse*
'For the best Drawings or Compositions of Ornaments taken from various prints, fit for Weavers [etc.] . . . by Boys under the Age of 15' (the subject generally to be taken from 'prints after Baptist'):
3rd: William Willis*
As above for 'Girls under the Age of 15':
2nd: Barbara Marsden
As above for 'Boys under the Age of 18':
4th: James Gandon: *a pattern for weavers**
'For the best Models in Clay of Figures, Busts, or Basso Relievos, by Youths under the Age of 22':
1st: Nathaniel Smith: *St. Andrew*
'For the best Models in Wax (fit for curious Artists in Gold, Silver, or other Metals) by Youths under the Age of 19':
1st: William Pars: *Cattle in a Landscape*
1759 'For the best Drawings of an Human Figure after Life, drawn at the Academy for Painting, etc., in St. Martin's Lane, by Youths under the Age of 24':
2nd: John Mortimer*
'For the best Drawings of any Statue, at the Candidate's own Election, in his Grace the Duke of Richmond's Collection, by Youths under the Age of 21':
1st: John Mortimer: *The Discobulus**
2nd: J. A. Gresse: *The Bacchus of Sansovino**
'For the best Drawings of an Human Figure or Figures, or Basso Relievos, from Models or Casts in Plaster, the principal Figure not under Twelve inches, by Youths under the Age of 22' (subject optional):

1st: Nathanel Smith: *Hercules and Atlas* after Roubilliac*
3rd: Joseph Nollekens: *Faun with Kid**†
4th: Richard Cosway: *Fighting Gladiator**
'For the best Drawings or Landscapes after Nature, by
Youths under the Age of 19':
3rd: James Gandon: *View of Paddington*
4th: William Pars: *Lambeth from Millbank Ferry**
For the best Drawings of Compositions after Nature, of
Beasts, Birds, Fruits or Flowers, by Youths under the Age
of 21':
Single Claim: Nathaniel Smith*†
'For the best Drawings of an Human Figure, after a Print
or Drawing, by Youths under the Age of 18' (general
subject *Bacchus* of any collection):
1st: J. A. Gresse: after Campigli
2nd: William Pars: *Bacchus of Sansovino*
3rd: Simon Taylor: the same
'For the best Drawings of any kind by Boys under the Age
of 14':
5th: William Willis: *An Academy Figure*
'For the best Drawings or Compositions of Ornaments,
being Original Designs fit for Weavers [etc.] . . . by Youths
under the Age of 18':
1st: William Pars
2nd: Simon Taylor
'For the best Models . . . in Clay, consisting of Birds,
Beasts, Fruit [etc.] . . . by Youths under the Age of 19':
2nd: William Hodges
'For the best Models in Wax [etc.] . . . by Youths under the
Age of 19':
1st: William Pars: *Flowers in Festoons*
'For the best Models in Clay of Figures, Busts or Basso
Relievos, by Youths under the Age of 22':
1st: Joseph Nollekens: *Abraham entertaining angels*
1760 'For the best Drawings of an Human Figure after Life
drawn at the Academy for Painting, etc., in St. Martin's
Lane, by Youths under the Age of 24':

1st: Richard Cosway

2nd: John Mortimer*

'For the best Drawings of a human Figure or Figures, from Models, Casts, or Basso Relievos . . . by Youths under the Age of 20 . . . to be made with Chalks only':

4th: William Parry: *The Dancing Faun**

'For the best Drawings of a Horse from the Life, by Youths under the Age of 20' (not less than 10 in. and in chalks):

1st: William Pars

'For the best Drawings of any Kind, human figures and heads excepted, by Boys under the Age of 14':

3rd: George Robertson: *A Horse from Life*

'For the best Models . . . in Clay, consisting of Birds, Beasts, Fruit [etc.] . . . by Youths under the Age of 19':

1st: Nathaniel Smith

'For the best Models in Clay, of Basso Relievos, by Youths under the Age of 25, being their own composition . . . [of] *Jephtha's rash vow*':

1st: Joseph Nollekens

1761: 'For the best Drawings of a Human Figure after the Life done at the Academy in St. Martin's Lane, by Youths under the Age of 24':

1st: John Mortimer

'For the best Drawings of any Statue, at the Candidate's own Election, in the Duke of Richmond's Gallery, by Youths under the Age of 21':

1st: J. A. Gresse: *Paetus and Arria*

'For the best Drawings of a human Figure or Figures from Models, Casts, or Basso Relievos . . . by Youths under the Age of 20 . . .':

1st: William Parry: *Hercules and Atlas*

'For the best Drawings or Compositions of Beasts or Birds from the Life . . . by Youths under the Age of 20':

1st: William Pars

As above, 'fit for Weavers [etc.] . . .':

1st: Simon Taylor

217

'For the best Drawings of a human Figure or Heads after
Drawings or Prints: by Youths under the Age of 16':
2nd: George Robertson: *An Academy Figure*
'For the best Drawings of any Kind (human Figures and
Heads excepted) by Boys under the Age of 14':
1st: George Robertson
'For the best Drawings of a Horse from the Life, by
Youths under the Age of 20' (not less than 10 in. and in
chalks):
2nd: George Robertson
'For the best Models in Clay . . . by Youths under the Age
of 22':
1st: Joseph Nollekens: *The Dancing Faun*
4th: Nathaniel Smith: *The Continence of Scipio*

[5]

MEMBERS OF THE SOCIETY OF ARTS
PROPOSED BY SHIPLEY

* The dates are of election to membership. Styles, addresses and
alphabetical sequence are as given in the MS. Sub. Books.
  † Corresponding Members. (Information relating to the proposal and
election of Corresponding Members has been extracted from MS. Trans.,
Dr. Templeman's, and Soc. Min.)

ANDERSON, Mr. Nicholas; Furnival's Inn Court, Holborn:
29th March 1758*
ASHBURNER, Mr. William, *Mercer*; Duke St., York Buildings:
19th November 1766
ASTLEY, Sir Edward, *Bt.*; Bath: 15th September 1756
BAILEY, Mr. William, *Organ Builder*; Corner Castle Court, Strand:
7th January 1756
BAKER, Mr. Jonathan, *Gent.*; New St., nr. Broad St., Soho:
2nd June 1762

BARNARD, Mr. Thomas Allen, *Merchant*; Holborn Bridge: 13th May 1761

BAISSIER, James, Esq.; Austin Fryars: 12th November 1760

BEASTAL, Mr. Leander, *Painter*; Gerrard St., Soho: 12th November 1760

BELCHIER, William, Esq.; Lombard St.: 4th February 1756

BOOTIE, Mr. John; Church Court, Strand: 16th March 1757

BRADSHAW, Thomas, Esq.; Treasury, Whitehall: 12th November 1760

BURCHETT, Mr. Samuel; St. Mary Hill: 14th November 1759

CARTWRIGHT, Edward, Esq.; Hatton Gdn., Holborn: 15th June 1757

COSWAY, Mr. Richard, *Artist*; Strand: 7th April 1762

DANKINS, James, Esq.; Brook St.: 7th April 1756

DELAVAL, Francis Blake, Esq.; Soho Sq.: 3rd January 1759

DELAVAL, John Hussey, Esq.: Soho Sq.: 3rd January 1759

DUNBAR, Mr. Robert; Aldermanbury: 5th November 1760

ETTINGTON, Mr. Israel, *Hosier*; Corner Lawrence Lane, Cheapside: 4th June 1760

EWER, Mr. Phileomen; Baseldon, Hants.: 30th November 1757

FANE, Francis, Esq.: Sackville St.: 12th March 1755

†FRANKLIN, Benjamin, Esq.; Philadelphia: 1st September 1756

FRITH, Mr. William; Jermyn St., St. James's: 21st December 1757

†GARDEN, Dr. Alexander; South Carolina: 5th March 1755

GERMAIN, Lady Betty; St. James's Sq.: 30th April 1755

GOADBY, Mr. Robert, *Merchant*; Sherborne, Dorset: 7th January 1756

GORDON, Mr. John; Kerry St., Golden Sq.: 8th February 1758

HANBURY, William, Esq.; Kelmarsh, Northants: 20th April 1757

HARCOURT, Simon, Earl; Cavendish Sq.: 14th April 1756

JENTY, Mr. Charles Nicholas; Bartlett's Buildings: 20th November 1760

LAWRENCE, Charles, Esq.; Essex St., Strand: 19th March 1760

†MADDEN, Rev. Dr. Samuel; Dublin: 13th April 1757

†MAIN, Mr. David; Scotland: 16th April 1755

MILDMAY, Carew, Esq.; Twyford, Hants: 20th October 1756

MILLER, Mr. James; Lombard St.: 28th April 1756

MILLER, William, Esq.; Queen's Row Pimlico; 16th April 1766

MOORE, Mr. Thomas, *Manufacturer*; Chiswell St.: 13th April 1757

MORRIS, Valentine, Esq.; Piercefield, Monmouth: 7th May 1760

ROBERTS, Mr. William, *Paper Manufacturer*; St. James's St.: 21st May 1760

RYLAND, Rev. Mr. John; Northampton: 1st August 1764

SAMWELL, Sir Thomas, Bt.; 11th June 1755

SHERLOCK, Mr. William; 19th March 1760

SIMMONS, Mr. James; Haselmere, Surrey: 21st May 1760

SKYRME, Francis, Esq.; Lyon's Inn: 18th July 1764

SMITH, Mr. Jaochim; Bow St., Covent Gdn.: 29th March 1758

STEVENS, Mr. Willoughby; Staines, Middlesex: 19th November 1755

TAYLOR, Mr. Joseph, *Stone Seal Engraver*; at the Eagles, Duke St., York Buildings: 20th April 1763

WAUGH, Mr. Joseph; Mercers Hall, Cheapside: 20th June 1759

WHITTY, Mr. Thomas; Axminster, Devon: 13th April 1757

WILLIS, Mr. William; Lombard St.: 1st October 1755

WOODFALL, Mr. George; Corner Craig's Court, Charing Cross: 1st October 1755

[6]

SHIPLEY'S ATTENDANCES AT COMMITTEES OF THE SOCIETY OF ARTS, 1760–87

'Notwithstanding particular Gentlemen are named for each Committee, every Member that shall please to attend is of every Committee' (*Rules and Orders of the Society of Arts*, 1758, pp. 14–15). Shipley was nominated in 1760 and 1761 to the Premium Committees, i.e. Agriculture, Chemistry, Colonies and Trade, Manufactures, Mechanics and Polite Arts, but not to the Administrative Committees—Accounts, Correspondence and Miscellaneous (Soc. Min., 12th November 1760 and 11th November 1761). His name does not appear in the nominations for subsequent years, though, as will be seen below, this did not prevent his attendance.

Session	Date of Meeting		Committee
1760–1	13th October	1760	Polite Arts
	18th		Polite Arts
	25th		Polite Arts
	18th November		Polite Arts
	25th		Polite Arts
	26th		Polite Arts
	18th December		Mechanics
	6th February	1761	Polite Arts
	20th		Polite Arts
	7th March		Chemistry
	19th		{ Chemistry / Polite Arts
	28th April		Polite Arts
	2nd June		Polite Arts
	16th		Polite Arts
	11th August		Correspondence
1761–2	20th November	1761	Mechanics
	3rd December		Mechanics
	24th		Mechanics
	7th January	1762	Mechanics
	15th		Accounts
	5th February		Polite Arts
	6th March		Mechanics
	11th		Polite Arts
	20th		Correspondence
	23rd		Polite Arts
	25th		Manufactures
	27th		Manufactures
	10th April		Polite Arts
	16th		Polite Arts
	29th		Polite Arts
	15th May		Polite Arts

Session	Date of Meeting		Committee
	21st		Polite Arts
	28th		Polite Arts
	3rd June		{ Polite Arts { Mechanics
	11th		Polite Arts
	14th		Polite Arts
	16th		Polite Arts
	17th		Polite Arts
	21st		Polite Arts
1762–3	5th July	1762	Polite Arts
	11th November		Mechanics
	12th		Chemistry
	19th		Polite Arts
	26th		Polite Arts
	3rd December		Polite Arts
	4th		Chemistry
	6th		Agriculture
	16th		Mechanics
	21st		Miscellaneous
	13th January	1763	Polite Arts
	24th		Polite Arts
	29th		Miscellaneous
	1st February		Miscellaneous
	8th		Mechanics
	18th		Polite Arts
	24th		Manufactures
	26th		Miscellaneous
	17th March		Polite Arts
	19th		Chemistry
	24th		Polite Arts
	26th		Mechanics
	1st April		Polite Arts
	2nd		Miscellaneous
	7th		Miscellaneous
	14th		Mechanics

Session	Date of Meeting		Committee
	15th		Polite Arts
	16th		Mechanics
	21st		Mechanics
	25th		Correspondence
	3rd May		Miscellaneous
	20th		Polite Arts
	9th June		Mechanics
1763–4	31st August	1763	Chemistry
	16th September		Polite Arts
	12th October		Chemistry
	18th November		Polite Arts
	25th		Polite Arts
	2nd December		Chemistry
	9th		Polite Arts
	16th		Polite Arts
	20th		Colonies
	22nd		Mechanics
	30th		Polite Arts
	3rd January	1764	Colonies
	6th		Polite Arts
	13th		Polite Arts
	20th		Polite Arts
	21st		Chemistry
	27th		Polite Arts
	3rd February		Polite Arts
	23rd		Manufactures
	26th		Correspondence
	1st March		Manufactures
	3rd		Chemistry
	9th		Polite Arts
	15th		Manufactures
	20th		Agriculture
	22nd		{ Manufactures { Mechanics
	26th		Polite Arts

Session	Date of Meeting		Committee
	30th		Polite Arts
	5th April		Mechanics
	6th		Mechanics
	9th		Mechanics
	14th		Mechanics
	19th		Mechanics
1764–5	11th July	1764	Chemistry
	26th		Mechanics
	21st December		Polite Arts
	8th March	1765	Polite Arts
	20th		Manufactures
	26th		{ Polite Arts { Agriculture
	6th April		Polite Arts
	8th		Polite Arts
	16th May		Mechanics
1765–6	29th October	1765	Colonies
	21st November		Mechanics
	25th		Agriculture
	29th		Polite Arts
	6th December		Polite Arts
	7th		Chemistry
	9th		Agriculture
	17th		Manufactures
	3rd January	1766	Polite Arts
	6th		Agriculture
	17th		Polite Arts
	18th		Chemistry
	24th		Polite Arts
	6th February		Mechanics
	8th		Manufactures
	14th		Polite Arts
	21st		Polite Arts
	27th		Mechanics

Session	Date of Meeting		Committee
	7th March		Polite Arts
	14th		Polite Arts
	20th		Polite Arts
	25th		Agriculture
	12th April		Miscellaneous
1766–7	12th January	1767	Agriculture
	30th		Polite Arts
	2nd February		Agriculture
1767–8	25th March	1768	Polite Arts
	5th April		Accounts
	22nd		Mechanics
1768–9	No attendances		
1769–70	No attendances		
1770–1	No attendances		
1771–2	28th April	1772	Mechanics
1772–3	No attendances		
1773–4	No attendances		
1774–5	No attendances		
1775–6	No attendances		
1776–7	No attendances		
1777–8	No attendances		
1778–9	19th November	1778	Mechanics
1779–80	No attendances		
1780–1	1st March	1781	Mechanics
	8th		Mechanics
	10th		Polite Arts
	5th April		Mechanics
	26th		Mechanics
1781–2	15th February	1782	Miscellaneous
1782–3	9th December	1782	Agriculture
	10th		Polite Arts

Q

Session	Date of Meeting		Committee
	19th		Mechanics
	1st April	1783	Miscellaneous
	4th		Miscellaneous
1783–4	No attendances		
1784–5	No attendances		
1785–6	30th January	1786	Agriculture
	6th February		Agriculture
	16th		Mechanics
	23rd		Mechanics
	26th May		Mechanics
	30th		Chemistry
1786–7	18th January	1787	Mechanics
	27th		Polite Arts
	1st February		Mechanics
	2nd		Polite Arts
	3rd		Miscellaneous
	5th		Agriculture
	17th May		Mechanics
	21st		Manufactures

[7]

FOUNDER MEMBERS OF THE KENTISH SOCIETY
(REPRINTED FROM THE 1786 *Proposal*. See *p*. 206)

* Subscribing Members.

*The Rt. Hon. Lord Romney.
*The Rt. Hon. Lord Fairfax.
Sir William Jones, one of
    the Supreme Judges in
    Bengal.

*The Hon. Charles Marsham,
    M.P.
*The Hon. and Rev. Jacob
    Marsham.
*Sir John Boyd, Bart.

*Gerrard Noel Edwards, Esq.,
   M.P.
*The Rev. William Davies
   Shipley, Dean of St. Asaph.
*Sir William Bishop, Knt.
— Allen, M.D.
Matthew Atkinson, Esq.
Mr. Thomas Baldock.
*John Brenchley, Esq.
*Mr. George Bishop.
*J. Calcraft, Esq.
*Mr. William Charles.
*The Rev. Mr. Cherry.
Mr. George Cockings.
Richard Cosway, Esq.
*Mr. Henry Creed.
*The Rev. Samuel Denne.
*Mr. Thomas Day.
*The Rev. Edward Frith.
Benjamin Franklin, LL.D.
Alexander Garden, M.D.
Mr. John Gibbons.
*Mr. John Golding.
Valentine Green, Esq.
*George Guy, Esq.
Edward Hasted, Esq.
Mr. Henry Hogben.
*Mr. Richard Holloway.
The Rev. John Howlett, A.M.
*Mr. William Jeffery.
Alexander Johnson, M.D.
*Mr. Charles Kite.
*Thomas Knight, Esq.

Mr. William Lashmire.
*Mr. John Latham.
*Mr. Thomas Latham.
*Mr. William Latham.
James Lind, M.D.
Charles Lempriere, Esq.
*Mr. George May.
Mr. John Mott.
Mr. James Mackie.
*John Mumford, Esq.
Donald Munro, M.D.
*William Pattenson, Esq.
The Rev. Mr. Pierson.
*William Philip Perren, Esq.
Thomas Pipon, Esq.
*Mr. Walter Prentis.
Mr. Robert Polhill, Surgeon,
   at Leghorn.
Mr. John Rose
Mr. Richard Samuel.
*Mr. John Simmons.
Mr. James Six.
*Mr. William Shipley.
*Mr. Thomas Smith.
*Mr. Flint Stacey.
*J. Thorpe, Esq.
*Mr. Edwin Turner.
The Rev. Mr. Samuel Weller.
Mr. — Walker.
*William Wheatly, Esq.
*The Rev. Dr. Whitfield.
*Mr. W. L. Williams.
Arthur Young, Esq.

BIBLIOGRAPHY AND ICONOGRAPHY

I. SHIPLEY MSS.

London:
British Museum: *Additional MSS*. Letters to Arthur Young and Sir Joseph Banks, 1786–8.
Linnean Society: Letter to the Society, 1796.
Royal Academy: *Humphry MSS*. Letter to Ozias Humphry, 1758.
Royal Society of Arts: *Minutes*. Rough Book, 1754–5. *Transactions*. Letters and memoranda addressed to the Society, 1776–87. *Guard Books*. Letters addressed to members of the Society and copies of Minutes and letters written on behalf of the Society, 1755. *Loose Archives*. Letters to the Society and to individual members, copies of Minutes, 1755–89.

Maidstone:
Museum and Art Gallery: *Shipley MSS*. Memoranda Books, 1758–88; Will, 1802. *Clement Taylor Smythe MSS*. Two fragments of letters re-used for memoranda c. 1795. *Hazlitt MSS*. Autographed trust deed, 1778.

Manchester:
John Rylands Library: *English MSS*. Letters to Henry Baker, 1747–53.

Philadelphia:
American Philosophical Society: *Franklin Papers*. Letters to Benjamin Franklin, 1755–6.

II. OTHER MS. SOURCES

London:
British Museum: *Sloane MSS*. *Whitley Papers* (Print Room).
New College, London: *Doddridge MSS*.
Royal College of Veterinary Surgeons: *Minutes of the Odiham Society*.

Royal Society: *Council Minutes. Miscellaneous MSS.*
Society of Antiquaries: *Minutes.*
Stationers' Hall: *Stationers' Company Records.*
Victoria and Albert Museum: *Forster Collection.*
Westminster Public Libraries; Archives Department: *Parish Rate Books.*

Maidstone:
Museum and Art Gallery: *J. M. Allchin's 'Lectures and Notes'. Brenchley Rent Book. Parish Rate Books.*

Twyford:
Twyford Moors: *Davies/Shipley family papers.*

Wilmington:
University of Delaware Library: *Margaret Hazlitt's 'Recollections'.*

III. PRINTED WORKS BY SHIPLEY
1753:

Proposals for raising by subscription a fund to be distributed in premiums for the promoting of improvements in the Liberal Arts and Sciences, Manufactures, etc. (See *pp.* 42–4.)

1753:
A Scheme for putting the Proposals in execution. (See *pp.* 44–6.)

1754:
To the Publick
The first notice issued by the Society of Arts. During the period of his Secretaryship, 1754–7, all its announcements were signed by Shipley. (See *pp.* 190–1.)

1757:
'Drawing in all its branches', etc. (Notice published in the *Public Advertiser*, 25th June 1757. (See *pp.* 80–1.)

1785:
'Account of the Use of a Floating Light', *Transactions of the Society of Arts*, Vol. III. (See *pp.* 93–5.)

1786:

A Proposal to establish a Society for promoting useful knowledge in the County of Kent. (See pp. 201–7.)

IV. PRINTED WORKS ON SHIPLEY

1   1763:

A concise Account of the Rise, Progress and Present State of the Society for the Encouragement of Arts, Manufactures, and Commerce, Instituted at London, Anno. MDCCLIV. Compiled from the Original Papers of the first Promoters of the plan; and from other authentic records. By a Member of the Said Society. (Generally attributed to Thomas Mortimer. In the introduction, p. iv, the author says the 'substance' of his narrative was based on a MS. by James Theobald deposited in the Society of Antiquaries. Theobald's MS. is no longer to be found.) Fullest and earliest account of Shipley's work as Founder of the Society of Arts, it contains the only known printed version of his 1753 pamphlets.

2   1803:

Joseph Moser, 'William Shipley': *European Magazine*, Vol. XLIV, pp. 176–8. Character sketch.

3   1808:

Edward Edwards, *Anecdotes of Painters*, p. xv. Brief note on Shipley as an artist and art teacher.

4   1839:

Topography of Maidstone, p. 41. Appears to be earliest printed reference to Shipley's work for the Kentish Society and his standing as a former celebrity of Maidstone.

5   1874:

Samuel Redgrave, *Dictionary of Artists of the English School*, p. 374, entry for Shipley as 'portrait and landscape painter', says he founded the St. Martin's Lane Academy (see also R. and S. Redgrave, *A Century of Painters of the English School*, 1866, Vol. I, p. 65 for the same confusion).

6   1881:

J. M. Russell, *The History of Maidstone*, pp. 285, 392. Extended version of information in 4.

7   1882:
H. B. Wheatley, 'William Shipley': *Jnl. S. of A.*, Vol. XXX, pp. 933–4, Brief note based on 6.

8   1897:
Thomas Seccombe, 'William Shipley': *Dictionary of National Biography*. Based on 5, 6 and 7.

9   1913:
Sir H. T. Wood, *The History of the Royal Society of Arts*, pp. 7–11. Fullest account to date. Uses 1, 5, 6 and 7.

10   1928:
W. T. Whitley, *Artists and Their Friends in England 1700–1799*, Vol. II, pp. 247–9. Uses 2.

11   1949:
K. W. Luckhurst, 'William Shipley and the Royal Society of Arts': *Jnl. R.S.A.*, Vol. XLVII, pp. 262–83. Sympathetic and perceptive account of Shipley's character and work as founder of the Society of Arts. Based on 1.

V. CHECK LIST OF AUTHORS CITED IN THE REFERENCES AND NOTES

Ackermann, R. FOUR (xi), 4.
Allen, R. J. ONE (b), 10.
Allot, R. W. ONE (a), 3.
Antal, F. ONE (b), 52.
Ashton, T. S. FIVE (xiv), 4.
Bailey, W. FOUR (x), 8.
Baker, H. TWO (iv), 7.
Bannerman, W. B. TWO (i), 3.
Becker, F. ONE (a), 13.
Bénézit, E. ONE (a), 13.
Berchtold, L. ONE (b), 54.
Berry, H. F. THREE (vi), 7.
Bourde, A. J. Documents 9, 3.
Bowden, W. ONE (b), 42.
Boys, J. FIVE (xvi), 18.
Bridgen, E. ONE (b), 21.

Bruce-Mitford, R. ONE (b), 16.
Bryan, M. ONE (a), 8.
Burney, W. FOUR (xii), 18.
Cannon, G. FIVE (xvi), 6.
Chambers, E. Documents 3, V, 1.
Chapman, J. FIVE (xiii), 3.
Christophersen, H. O. FIVE (xv), 1.
Clark-Kennedy, A. E. THREE (vi), 6.
Clay, R. S. Documents 3, III, 1.
Court, T. H. Documents, 3, III, 1.
Cox Johnson, A. THREE (vii), 3

Cunningham, W. ONE (b), 42.

Cust, Sir L. ONE (b), 13.

Day, T. FIVE (xiii), 24.

Dossie, R. TWO (ii), 4.

Edmunds, M. FOUR (viii), 13.

Edwards, E. TWO (ii), 2.

Edwards, M. B. FIVE (xv), 12.

Ernle, Lord. Documents 9, 2.

Evans, J. ONE (b), 11.

Farington, J. FIVE (xvi), 19.

Franklin, B. Documents 7, 5.

Froom, F.J. TWO (i), 9.

Girouard, M. ONE (b), 50.

Grant, M. H. TWO (ii), 6.

Gunther, R. T. Documents 3, I, 1.

Gwynn, J. ONE (b), 51.

Hans, N. ONE (b), 14.

Hanson, L. W. ONE (b), 3.

Hartley, Sir H. ONE (b), 17.

Hayward, H. ONE (b), 43.

Hill, Sir J. ONE (b), 30.

Hooke, R. Documents 3, I, 1.

Humphreys, J. D. Documents 3, II, 3.

Jones, M. G. ONE (b), 56.

Jones, T. FOUR (xi), 9.

Kelly, T. ONE (b), 11.

Kenyon, K. M. R. TWO (i), 7.

Labaree, L. W. FIVE (xvi), 8.

Lillywhite, B. TWO (ii), 12.

Locke, J. FIVE (xv), 1.

McLachlan, H. TWO (iii), 12.

Madden, S. THREE (v), 8.

Melville, R. L. FOUR (x), 12.

Middleton, J. H. Documents 3, VI, 1.

Montesquieu, C. L. de S. de. FIVE (xvi), 14.

Mortimer, T. TWO (ii), 4.

Mulvany, T. J. FOUR (xi), 2.

Namier, Sir L. FOUR (viii), 3.

Nash, T. R. Documents 3, VIII, 2.

Nef, J. U. THREE (v), 6.

Nichols, J. TWO (i), 7.

Page, W. TWO (i), 11.

Peck, P. ONE (b), 35, 36.

Phillips, H. THREE (vii), 4.

Pope, A. FIVE (xv), 9.

Portus, G. V. ONE (b), 9.

Postlethwait, M. ONE (b), 5.

Prescott, J. A. Documents 9, 3.

Pyne, W. H. TWO (ii), 9.

Reinach, S. Documents 3, VII, 1.

Robinson, E. ONE (a), 5.

Rogers, J. E. T. THREE (v), 4.

Roget, J. L. FOUR (xi), 11.

Schofield, R. E. ONE (a), 3.

Schuyler, R. L. THREE (v), 7.

Shadwell, T. ONE (b), 32.

Smith, A. THREE (v), 8.

Smith, Sir J. E. FOUR (viii), 7.

Smith, J. T. FOUR (xi), 1.

Sprat, T. ONE (b), 24.

Stedman, T. THREE (vii), 11.

Stimson, D. ONE (b), 26.

Stukeley, W. Documents 3, VIII, 1.

Teignmouth, Lord. FIVE (xvi), 3.

Thieme, U. ONE (a), 13.

Trengrove, L. ONE (b), 32.

Tucker, J. THREE (v), 7.
Tucker, N. FIVE (xvi), 15.
Turberville, A. S. FIVE (xv), 1.
Vertue, G. TWO (ii), 9.
Walpole, H. ONE (b), 30.
Waterhouse, E. TWO (ii), 3.
Weld, C. R. Documents 3, II, 2.

Whatley, S. TWO (iii), 1.
Wheatley, H. B. ONE (b), 18.
Whitley, W. T. TWO (ii), 3.
Williams, B. ONE (b), 46.
Williamson, G. C. FOUR (x), 17.
Yarrantion, A. ONE (b), 2.
Young, A. FIVE (xv), 3.

VI. PERIODICAL PUBLICATIONS USED

Annals of Agriculture
Annals of Science
Brycheiniog
Country Life
Engineering
European Magazine
Flintshire Historical Society (Jnl.)
Gentleman's Magazine
Kentish Gazette
Kentish Society (Trans.)
Monthly Magazine
Northampton Mercury
Philosophical Transactions
Public Advertiser
Society of Arts (Trans. and Jnl.)
The Spectator
The Tatler
Walpole Society (Annual Vols.)

VII. PORTRAITS OF SHIPLEY*

1. *By John Smart,* 1757
In chalks. Whereabouts unknown.
Gained the first premium of the Society of Arts 'for the best
Drawings by Boys under the Age of 17' (see R. Dossie, *Memoirs of*

* See also list of illustrations *p.* vii. above.

Agriculture, Vol. III, p. 399).

2. *By Richard Cosway, c.* 1759–60

Half length in oils. In 1760 Exhibition of works of living artists. Presented to the Society by the artist in 1785 through the intervention of Caleb Whitefoord (see Whitley, Vol. II, pp. 247–8).

3. *By James Barry,* 1778

Full length, sitting, in oils: part of group of figures in 'The Society'. See Barry, *An Account of a Series of Pictures in the Great Room of the Society of Arts,* 1783, p. 72.

4. *By William Hincks,* 1786

Quarter length, miniature watercolour on ivory.

Presented to the Society in 1786 by the artist but subsequently lost. Recovered in 1924 through the kindness of Herbert Monckton of Maidstone, whose sister was said to have received it from Mrs. William Peale in 1866 (see *Jnl. R.S.A.,* Vol. LXXIII, 1925, pp. 26–8). But this may be the copy which Shipley's daughter, Elizabeth Peale, had made by Christopher Barber in 1803 (see Soc. Min., 30th March 1803).

5. *By William Hincks,* 1786

Copper-plate engraving of 4 (see *Transactions,* Vol. IV, 1786, frontispiece and p. xviii).

INDEX